THE OTTAWA SCHOLAR

VOLUME TWO
2021
EDITED BY
JUSTIN CLARKE, PH.D.

urbanpress

The Ottawa Scholar-Volume Two, 2021
Edited by Justin Clarke, Ph.D.
Copyright ©2021 Ottawa University

ISBN 978-1-63360-171-0

All rights reserved. This book is protected under the copyright laws of the United States of America. This book may not be copied or reprinted for commercial gain or profit.

For Worldwide Distribution
Printed in the U.S.A.

Urban Press
P.O. Box 8881
Pittsburgh, PA 15221-0881
412.646.2780
www.urbanpress.us

TABLE OF CONTENTS

	PREFACE	V
	INTRODUCTION	VII
	SPECIAL INTRODUCTION	IX
	FROM DR. REGGIES WENYIKA	
SECTION ONE	HANNAH DEWARE	2
	KARLEY FAUDERE	5
	JONATHAN FOX	8
	YAN KEUWO	11
	ELI OWINGS	14
SECTION TWO	KAYLEN ASHLEY	18
	BRODY BURKHOLDER	22
	OTIS COSTLOW	26
	JESSAMINE GREUTER	30
	COLLIN HANSON	32
	LAWSON MEDLEN	36
	DERRIANE MORRISON	40
SECTION THREE	TRENTON BARROWS	44
	ANGEL GARRETT	49
	BRYNDEN GROW	54
	DOMINIC WIMBUSH	59
SECTION FOUR	JOE CORBIN	64
	MEGHAN CUBBISON	70
	LUKE GRAHAM	92
	ABIGAIL MEYER	99
	ALLISON RIVERS	108
	HANNAH O. SAUCEDA	114
	WILLIAM WALLACE	120
	CONCLUSION	125

PREFACE

Welcome to Volume Two of *The Ottawa Scholar* in which we showcase contributions from the Ottawa University Scholars Program students. The students are prompted to submit written responses to various questions and their responses differ progressively by year or classification. The specifics are explained elsewhere in this edition.

I'm very proud of this initiative since it gives some of our best and brightest the opportunity to express themselves and to explain their choice of and the impact of Ottawa University in their lives. This is the work of students at different levels and milestones of their career and journeys toward personal significance. Read it as such and enjoy this edition as you did last year's inaugural edition which was well received. Copies were distributed to many of the University's constituents and the feedback was quite positive. Allow me to share with you a note I received from an alumna of the university who is also on the board of trustees and chairs its academic affairs committee:

> *"Just a note to thank you for sending The Ottawa Scholar. I thoroughly enjoyed reading it, and I have to say that some of the essays brought tears to my eyes. I identified so much with the emotions expressed by the freshmen—the uncertainty, the longing to fit in, and so many adjustments they found challenging just as I did.*
>
> *The writings of the upperclass students were so much more sophisticated and were also less personal. They displayed greater confidence in their opinions and feelings. I found it fascinating to see the emerging maturity year-by-year. The fact that almost all the students felt, many immediately, that they had found a home at OU was something I also experienced."* – Pam Woodward, class of 1970.

Thank you for supporting our students, Pam. I am also especially grateful to Menard Family Professor of Philosophy and Ethics, Dr. Justin Clarke, for his work as director of our Scholars Program and editor of *The Ottawa Scholar*. Throughout the year, he teaches, meets with, challenges, and intellectually coaches the students. His tireless efforts, especially during a year impacted by a global pandemic, are greatly appreciated.

Reggies Wenyika, Ed.D.
President & Professor of Education and Religion
Ottawa University
Ottawa, Kansas
July of 2021

INTRODUCTION

Time flies and now our second volume of *The Ottawa Scholar* is finished. What an odd year we have experienced and what an interesting edition of *The Ottawa Scholar* you have in your hands. The submissions for this volume reflect the fractured state of the world, and our students admirably and honestly discuss the challenges of excelling both in and out of the classroom. They faced novel obstacles and opportunities in 2020-2021, and their determination will inspire you as it does me.

As I write, we appear to be emerging out of the more severe aspects of the pandemic lockdown. I'm hopeful we'll be able to get back to living, working, and flourishing sooner rather than later but only time will tell if that is a forecast or wishful thinking. I want to thank the administration at Ottawa for making some bold choices early on, one of them their commitment to keep Ottawa as open as possible in the 2020-2021 school year, while permitting students and faculty to work remotely if they chose to do so. Many of the students and faculty I spoke with relished the chance to be physically back in the classroom in the fall of 2020 after spending so much time during the spring of 2020 involved in distance learning. I am grateful for that opportunity to connect with students and colleagues alike.

I hope this volume will serve as a valuable possession for our scholars throughout their lives. For now, our young scholars may use this book to look ahead to what their older counterparts are feeling as they complete and look forward to their graduation. In the future, hopefully all our scholars will read this to look back and reflect so they can be reminded of their focus and struggles during this time of their lives.

Finally, I think this book would be of interest to students who consider attending Ottawa University as they wonder what the life of the mind looks like here. I can think of no better portrait of the potential that awaits our incoming students than this glimpse into the world of our Ottawa Scholars. Our Scholars are bright, motivated, promising, and courageous. They have exciting futures ahead of them and are poised to lead lives of significance. If you don't believe me, then read what they have written for yourself and once you do, I am sure you will agree.

Dr. Justin Clarke
Menard Family Professor of Philosophy and Ethics
Director, Ottawa Scholars Program
Ottawa University Midwest
July of 2021

SPECIAL INTRODUCTION

LEADING THROUGH UNCERTAINTIES:

REFLECTIONS FROM THE COVID-19 PANDEMIC

DR. REGGIES WENYIKA

DISRUPTIONS TO HIGHER EDUCATION

The higher education industry has known for a while that its future will not look anything like its past. During the last four decades, the industry has endured, adapted to, and in some cases incited disruptions that realized or resulted in the massification of college or post-secondary education. Disruptions in the higher education industry have included the rapid expansion into online education and the ensuing advent of the Massive Open Online Courses (MOOCs) phenomenon. We also saw the rise of the for-profit higher education sector accompanied by an unprecedented marketing and advertising tidal wave that capitalized on the spike in adult enrollments after the post-911 global financial crisis, and to a lesser extent, the 2007-2008 financial crisis.

ENTER: THE COVID-19 PANDEMIC

It goes without saying that the pandemic affected many organizations. For higher education, the impact was on our modus operandi and financial models. Some colleges wondered if they would ever be able to fill their dorm rooms, classrooms, and dining and campus cafeterias. When the pandemic started, none of us knew what the impact was going to be on college athletics—but we assumed the worst and we were not far off. Back then, the normal for which we were yearning would have been what our colleges looked like in the year prior to the pandemic.

Earlier in the Spring of 2020, when we switched to a distance education modality as did many colleges in America, Ottawa University had the technological infrastructure and online/distance education capabilities to do so. However, not many were prepared for the scale and suddenness of the shift and the surprising results. Why? We were not ready because of a seemingly counterintuitive reason. The members of what's known as Generation Z (GenZ) are digital natives who have lived in that world for their entire lives. Naturally, it followed that they would take to online education like ducks to water. This was an understandable assumption made by many, including yours truly. That turned out *not* to be the case. Regardless, as we were looking to the fall of 2020, some institutions took preemptive and somewhat drastic measures.

For example, during the summer of 2020, the California State University System, the largest in the nation, made the decision to close all its institutions for the fall of 2020. We all wondered if this was going to have a ripple effect across America, especially in states like Kansas There is such a thing as peer pressure among institutions and their leaders. Nobody wants to be known as the first to dive into what will turn out to be a mistake, and nobody wants to be known as the last one out of the same pool. At Ottawa University, in the state of Kansas, we took a stand and made a bold decision. We decided we were going to have normal face-to-face classroom sessions, starting the fall semester two weeks earlier than usual. The decision was questioned by some and second guessed by others. We may not have had all the answers, but we were never in doubt as to what our students expected of us and that was to provide them a quality education they had come to expect along with a vibrant campus student life. All this had to occur while keeping everyone healthy and safe. I was blessed to be surrounded by a dedicated and courageous team who jumped into the water first and made it happen, even though there were not many models or paths to follow that had been forged by other institutions.

We also decided to administer a COVID-19 test to all students when they returned to campus while instituting the recommended precautionary guidelines. We hit some bumps along the way, but we successfully delivered on our promises to students and completed the academic year successfully. The lesson learned and lived is that leaders make values-based decisions that do not depend on the environment. In the late 1980s, we were introduced to the concept of VUCA leadership. VUCA is an acronym for Volatile, Uncertain, Complex, and Ambiguous, and there will be times when leaders are faced with VUCA times, and come what may, they are expected to lead and navigate through such times. The pandemic was a great case study of a VUCA environment.

My contention is that as a leader in higher education, or in any sector for that matter, one must maintain the ability to reinvent oneself. Institutions are no different, for over time they have had to adapt to the different generations walking through their doors. Most will remember how we began this millennium and century. Colleges were chiefly led and managed by Baby Boomers and Generation Xers as they sought to educate and influence Generation Y, otherwise labeled the Millennials. The Boomers have and are in the process of retiring, and Gen Y has since graduated. The next generations are now in charge, educating Generation Z, the denizens of the digital world. We are learning progressively and rather rapidly that GenZ citizens needs and perspectives about college education are quite different than their predecessors.

Overall, higher education has in the past met these changes with appropriate innovative responses and timely adaptations. However, the changes and previous disruptions pale in comparison to the COVID-19 pandemic. For all intents and purposes, the pandemic has been a game-changer. It has shaken our foundations and left us asking questions that we have never asked before, questions to which we have yet to develop intellectually or administratively satisfying answers:

1. Will there ever be such a thing as normal? Some have postulated that as the pandemic subsides, we will return to normal. Some have opted for the phrase *new normal*. What exactly is normal? What is the new normal? Going forward, is normal a transitional construct that can be easily defined and widely accepted? Will it unfold as quickly as the pandemic did or will it require more time?

2. As a higher education leader, what do I need to do to prepare GenZ for the future world they are going to, one that is based on ideas and things that none of us have seen or ever experienced?

3. What and when will the next disruption be and what will be the intensity of its impact on personal lives and the higher education industry?

4. We know how the state and the federal government responded at the onset of the pandemic and during the pandemic to mitigate its impact on citizens and institutions. How will they respond in the future, and will they have the means and willingness to buoy the economy, institutions, and individuals as they did in 2020?

5. We now know that in certain sectors and jobs, it is possible to work from home and still be a highly productive employee. To what extent has that changed the structure of jobs and employment, or the nature of work? What does this all mean for college education and how we prepare students for a future in which working from home may be the standard or new normal?

Why did I even ask myself such questions in the first place? It is because like many, I have a sense that this disruption was unique, and that there is some permanency to its effects and our responses. Why was this one different?

The pandemic caught many countries and communities unprepared. This challenge was further compounded by the politicization of communication processes and responses. Though the world had dealt with aerosolized viruses before for decades, COVID's virulence and pathogenicity was extraordinary. Institutions over the years have successfully dealt with such infections as SARS coronavirus (CoV), Norovirus, H1N1, bacterial meningitis, influenza A/B, MRSA, and Hepatitis A. However, COVID-19 presented a significantly higher infection risk.

Additionally, infections rose at a time when the global energy market was in turmoil, thus creating a perfect storm for economic misery. As we emerge from the pandemic, the hot topic now is vaccination. We are past the availability issue and currently dealing with hesitancy or reluctance to submit to any notion of a mandatory edict. As of this writing, the message we have sent to our students is that we expect members of our community to be vaccinated. It is not a matter of politics or personal preference, but a matter of looking after oneself, their neighbor, and their community.

WHAT LESSONS HAVE WE LEARNED THAT WE CAN PASS ON TO FUTURE GENERATIONS?

So, what does this mean for the future of college education? It means everything and nothing. It means everything because as leaders we are having to escalate our out-of-the-box thinking in terms of schedules, delivery, funding, and structure. Ottawa University is actively engaged in this process. We are considering how we can best leverage some of our business, nursing, and engineering offerings to meet the needs of local and regional families and business entities. How best can local industry benefit from the services Ottawa University has to offer? We are not alone in this challenge. The next few years will see a rise in innovative pedagogies along with the rise of new college models.

It means nothing because the value of a college education is not likely to change. An April 17, 2020, *Forbes* ran an article written by one of their contributors entitled, "College Graduates Are Less Likely to Become Unemployed Due To The Coronavirus." This is yet another vindication of the value that a college education adds to an individual's economic prospects. Those who held college degrees were, statistically, less likely to be laid off during the pandemic. A college education is still and will continue to be a reliable means for stabilizing an individual's economic prospects and serve as a portal for their quest to find a fulfilling life and achieve upward social mobility. However, this does not mean that colleges should not adapt to or anticipate new realities.

One would hope that the pandemic has presented colleges with an opportunity for organizational introspection. One thing is clear, however, and that is things are never going to be the same. College education, though it remains the same in essence, will not look the same as it did in yesteryear. The pandemic has exposed some of the outdated and obsolete economic and modality assumptions that we have held to for years. That said, the good news is that college education is here to stay—and so is Ottawa University.

I am particularly pleased with our Scholars Program since Ottawa University is a college that pursues its objectives from the perspective of the traditional liberal arts. An answer to all the questions I asked myself earlier in this writing may actually be enhancing the liberal arts. The liberal arts is an answer for the future in that it gives students the requisite foundation, life skills, and thinking tools to help them adapt, engage, and effectively function in an ever-changing and increasingly diverse world. While we are not expecting all our scholars to emerge from Ottawa University as public intellectuals, we do expect them to develop the ability to communicate, think, synthesize, and appropriately frame contemporary issues and occurrences in their proper historical and philosophical context, regardless of their chosen discipline. We at Ottawa University believe that is the best means to prepare leaders for a world we have yet to experience let alone comprehend.

SECTION ONE

FIRST QUESTION
"Why did you choose Ottawa University? What are you most looking forward to during your Ottawa experience?"

In the past, a majority of our students chose Ottawa after a process that involved visiting multiple college campuses before deciding Ottawa was the best fit. In last year's *Ottawa Scholar*, many students noted that spending time on Ottawa's campus helped them make the decision to commit. Most students in the Fall of 2020 incoming class didn't get to participate in that particular rite of passage. That was because their senior year of high school was cut short by the pandemic and colleges across the U.S. suspended visitation in March of 2020. Those students who had not chosen a school by then had to do with less information or hands-on experience. It's interesting to read our scholars describe this process since it is unlike anything I went through. I hope that the situation isn't the new normal for college admissions. I'm pleased our admissions department has resumed on-site visitation so future incoming classes won't face that limitation again.

This window into our scholars' lives in this section is fascinating, and they deserve our respect and admiration. They did something that was both difficult and brave: They made a commitment in the face of a global uncertainty that people they knew could neither remember experiencing nor could predict how it would all play out.

HANNAH DEWARE

Like every other high school senior in the class of 2020, I was left holding an empty bag for graduation with a diploma delivered as a PDF. With this very swift end of my high school experience because of a worldwide pandemic, I was left wondering, "What's next?" I pondered the age-old question I was often asked as I grew up, "What did I want to do with my life when I grew up?"

Ready or not, it was time for a decision for I truly was "grown up." I had constantly bounced around with many different ideas of a future profession, including (but not limited to) genetic engineering, physiology, and education. The common theme through all of them seemed to be that I wanted to create a better future for those I leave behind. When the time came for me to apply for colleges and research scholarships, I had finally settled on education as my focus. I knew I wanted to continue my education *for* education because of my need to better the world around me. In other words, I wanted to have a life of significance.

My experience applying for colleges and scholarships was different, to say the least, because I couldn't experience a normal campus tour or obtain an understanding of student life because of the prevailing pandemic. Ironically and unknowingly, I missed the deadline to compete in the scholarship competition, the very Scholars Program for which I write this essay. Ottawa University had always been on my radar of college choices. Both of my father's parents and both of my parents attended and graduated from Ottawa (both sets also married while attending Ottawa as well).

Yet even armed with this knowledge and family history, I was locked in an internal struggle concerning where to enroll for my teaching degree as the Fall quickly approached. In the end, I whittled my choices down to two universities. Both options had many benefits and seemed to be a good fit for me. Even the cost of attending would be the same because of different scholarships I had been offered.

My choice to attend Ottawa University was made by one simple phone call. In the midst of COVID-19's insanity and figuring out my next step, Ottawa was the only college to call and check in on how I was doing. They didn't do this for selfish reasons to persuade me to attend or to rush my decision-making process. Someone simply wanted to make sure I was doing okay.

At Ottawa, I am not simply a student ID number or a dollar sign.

I am a real breathing person with life goals that will lead to a life of significance. The further I pursued Ottawa as my top choice in education, the more these facts were presented to and confirmed for me. I was not, and still am not, just another face in a crowded classroom.

Once I arrived, I dove into the student culture looking for options of where to spend my time and I was yet again shown that the university and its staff care about my interests. I was introduced to the women's soccer team, where I swiftly started training and bettering my physical body, and joined the forensics and debate team, where I quickly grew in my knowledge of the workings of today's society. Both of these activities broadened my worldview and are making me a better person—and that after only one single semester!

Obviously, I look forward to continuing my education and then to achieve my dream job, but the implications of this journey are just as exciting. From a young age, my parents instilled in me a love for learning, and any new knowledge is fascinating to me—no matter the subject. The practice of this would seem simple enough. I attend classes and do my homework as, in theory, any successful student would. However, this isn't what I look forward to the most.

I have good study habits and I know what keeps my attention for classes; these are disciplines I have already achieved. I look forward to expanding my social life, and I know I sound like the stereotypical college student who says something like this, but it is the truth and comes from the life of a nerd. I am a self-proclaimed extrovert who due to the pandemic has lost significant social skills, ones I am in desperate need of for my future profession. With safety regulations in place and mask in hand, I was able to once again find these social skills through the relations and organizations I am a part of at Ottawa.

Clearly my freshmen year has had a lot of rough patches and my transition to university life was one that quite honestly took a physical and mental toll on me. I burned myself out quickly and for the first time I didn't have the safety nets to catch me as I did at home. I was seriously struggling with my own mental health and didn't see the value I once had in my own education.

The good news is that Ottawa had just the help I needed. I just hadn't discovered it yet. The University has resources and people available who are willing and capable of helping any student whether it's someone in desperate need, like I was, or a person in need of a simple and friendly chat with a needy student. It was armed with these resources that I returned home with a more realistic outlook on myself, my education and life in general.

With this much-needed assistance from the Ottawa family of professionals, I was able to once again recognize the value in my education that I had lost sight of for a brief period of time. Now on the other side of this struggle, I have emerged with a much stronger sense of my value in and direction for my education and subsequent life of significance.

The reason I mention all of this is simple: The struggles I overcame made me look forward to the things to come, for both my time here at Ottawa University and my life afterwards. As I mentioned before, I've only completed one semester here at Ottawa, yet one semester is enough to teach me that I have found a real beginning at the right place for my life of significance.

Hannah Deware is a freshman from Atchison, Kansas. She is a member of the women's soccer team and Forensics and Debate Team. Hannah is currently double majoring in secondary education in English and secondary education in speech and theater and will graduate in 2024. After graduation, Hannah plans on heading into teaching while furthering her education with a master's degree as she gathers real-world experience in the classroom.

KARLEY FAUDERE

    I could easily write a paper about how I visited Ottawa University and felt at home and at peace with my decision to attend. I could answer this question by describing how Ottawa was simply the place I belonged, but I will not do that. Ottawa did not call my name, did not have everything I wanted in a school, and did not fit the picture in my mind of what my future would be—or where I would be creating it. For years, as I watched friends go off to college and as I visited college campuses myself, many times I heard the phrase "It just felt like home." The truth is that nothing felt like home to me—no college felt like the perfect fit.

    I graduated high school in the midst of a worldwide pandemic, I visited colleges that were halfway shut down, and I found no life on any campus. How was any college going to feel like home when not a single school had the ability to show me who they were? So, yes, I could write the age-old, sappy story about how Ottawa is my home and how I could never imagine myself anywhere else, but any choice I could have made about college was going to sound more like a business deal than a home. Ottawa may not feel like home yet, but I chose to come here because I felt like there was more opportunity available to me.

    My dreams are huge and unbelievably specific, so therefore not many schools fit the bill. Big dreams require long journeys, and I knew Ottawa University would be my first step. I plan to become a doctor of genetics. In this role, I will work with individuals who have genetic disorders in the hopes of reducing the handicaps that exist in the everyday life of genetically affected people through the use of medicine and genetic therapy techniques as well as new and evolving treatments.

    As I set out to pick a school for my undergraduate degree, I knew I would need professors who had connections and the capability to prepare me for not only medical school but also for a life in an understudied field. I knew I needed the resilience to keep learning for the rest of my life, and for that to happen I needed to enjoy learning. The professors at Ottawa made me feel like this could be a place to learn everything I need to know and to be excited about doing so. They spoke of multiple projects that were underway with senior research and of future ideas for genetics-linked projects. As I sat in the room on my visit and listened to them talk, I got excited about being able to learn and to discover new topics with the information the professors would teach me. I was excited for a future I already knew I would love.

Academics was not my only expectation from the school I would attend. I love to play basketball and I love to play the violin. It is possible to play the violin without an orchestra, but it is difficult to play basketball without a team. Ottawa offered me the opportunity to play the game I love for four more years. I am not a Division One athlete and I am not going to play basketball for the rest of my life, but I will play for as long as I can. Four more years of doing something I love is a gift I simply could not pass up. Every day I wake up to go to practice, I remember how blessed I am to have gotten this opportunity many others have not. Basketball is exhausting, difficult, and draining but it is also exactly what I wanted to do for as long as possible.

I took a gamble and signed to play on a team without a coach. I had no clue who would be coaching me day in and day out. That gamble paid off and I get to show up to the gym and get better every day under a coach whom I respect. My coach has so much to teach me and she does so with a heart that reflects a Christian faith. Her practices can be hard on the body and mind. I may feel like I want to quit sometimes but then I remember that I love the game, I love my team, and I love my coaches. There is truly no better way to learn than from people you respect, look up to, and can grow spiritually because of. I cannot say that I chose Ottawa because of my coach but I can say that she is one of the reasons I will continue to attend here.

Ottawa does not have an orchestra, but they offered me the opportunity to have individual lessons. Any form of growth as a musician was a selling point for me. If I could learn more, I was happy to do so in any way possible. I love the violin course I take at Ottawa and was correct in thinking it would help me as a musician. I have learned how to focus on technical issues and pinpoint them rather than constantly preparing for concerts and performances. I was hesitant to go to a school without an orchestra because I was worried it might stunt my growth as a musician but attending Ottawa has done the opposite.

During the remainder of my time here, I am looking forward to many things. I am looking forward to growing as a student, a person, an athlete, and a musician. I believe the only endeavor worthwhile in life is growth. If I am constantly growing in all of the areas of my life, then I am bettering myself and the world around me. What more could I hope for than a life that is better because of the effort I put into my self-development? Ottawa may not have been my dream and it may not have been home, but Ottawa is my current step in my pursuit of growth. Ottawa offered me a world of opportunity which I will not take for granted.

Karley Faudere is a freshman from Eldorado, Kansas. She is a member of the Ottawa women's basketball team and a devoted musician. Upon graduation, she plans to apply to medical school.

JONATHAN FOX

My college search got off to a strong start when I was accepted into nearly every school to which I applied. I didn't shoot for the stars and apply to Harvard, but I did apply to several local schools where I was accepted. I knew I wanted a place close to home and Ottawa is just twenty minutes away, and I also knew I did not want to go to a huge school where the teachers know you by a number. I wanted the teachers to know my name and treat me like a person. I wanted a school that had areas for the students to gather and play games like pool, ping pong, or air hockey. And I wanted to go to a school where the students had a voice in what happens on campus.

I also wanted to play football in college because of the second family that it builds among the participants. I have also been playing football since third grade, so I have always been around the sport. In high school, I was always on the field because our team was small, once having only 15 players on the entire roster. I went on several tours of the campus and when I went on the visit day for football, I got to see the weight and training room and I knew this was the football program for me.

I had only played on a turf field a couple of times because my high school field was grass and had a big mound in the middle of it. Our practice field used to be a cow pasture, so to be fair, all of the college football fields looked amazing to me. Trying to find the right school was pretty hard because I did not get a fitting or usual end to my senior year. I was really excited to play ball and when spring break hit, I thought there was no way that COVID would get big enough to keep us out of school. The graduation held for my class was outdoors drive-in style and while it was memorable, it did not feel like a proper end to high school.

The only offer I received to play college football was from Ottawa. This was a little discouraging, but I still went and met with Coach Kent Kessinger and was relieved that he knew about a scholarship that I could try and get. This scholarship would pay for full tuition all four years of college. I would have to live on campus, but that was just fine with me. I was a little worried about roommates and if the cafeteria food was any good, but all of these worries were put rest almost as fast as they arose.

The scholarship I am referencing is The Franklin County High Achiever Scholarship. There was a little bit of a competition for this scholarship that involved writing an essay and answering questions from a panel. I was really nervous because I knew if I did not get this scholarship, then chances were that I would not be attending college at all. I was fortunate that in the previous weeks, I had been learning public speaking and had gone over learned helplessness—which is the topic that I chose for my paper.

The question that had to be answered in the paper was, "What problems do you see in the modern school system and how can we fix it?" During the panel of questions, I was freaking out and my heart was beating out of my chest, but the whole time I was able to stay calm on the outside and keep putting together good answers to the questions presented. The days following the competition were stressful as I kept reviewing what I could have done differently to improve my chances. When I was walking down the stairs and the competition was over, I was quite relieved because I knew I had given it my all. When I got into the car with my parents, I knew I had done all that I could and my best to answer all the questions they had—as well as all of the questions still running through my head.

When I found out that I got the scholarship because then I knew I could actually go to college. I let my parents know and of course they shared the excitement. I did not think I would actually win the scholarship, but I feel so blessed to have received it.

Ottawa was a school I never really considered at first, but ended up falling in love with it the second I saw the campus and got a look inside the football program. I knew it was going to be a little strange playing football without a football scholarship, but I knew I wanted to try it. I knew it was going to be an entirely different experience then high school and I was about to work harder than I ever had before—but I did not really care. I had a couple people tell me that I wouldn't be able to do it and to just do the school, but I wanted to prove all of those people wrong.

Now with my first semester out of the way, it is safe to say I made the right decision. I have met some great people I gladly call my friends and all of my professors know my name. This school, while it might not look like a whole lot, has everything I could need and want from a college. And while I may live close to my actual family, I know I have built a strong relationship with the football team and I gladly call them my second family, my football brothers.

Jonathan Fox is a freshman from Richmond, Kansas and is a member of the Braves football team. Jonathan is majoring in business and plans to graduate in 2024. He does not yet know exactly what he wants to do after graduation.

YAN KEUWO

As I entered my senior year of high school, I was still unsure of my future. I didn't know what major I wanted to pursue or the place at which I would pursue this yet-to-be decided major. Even the future of my athletic career was in question, as the love I once had for football was dwindling. As the year progressed, not much changed in my mindset until the conclusion of my senior season of football.

I had believed up to that point that it would be the last time I would put on a jersey. It didn't take long for me to realize that football meant much more to me than I had admitted to myself. When I first began playing, it was to have fun and make friends. As my experience deepened, however, the original motivation had dissipated only to be replaced with the winning mentality.

My mind had been infiltrated with the idea that if you weren't winning, the sport couldn't or wouldn't be enjoyable. This reasoning was the main cause that led to my my high school football career being miserable. At the conclusion of the season unlike many of my teammates, no tears were shed. It didn't really feel like there was much to miss or regret about my entire high school football career. My team never won more than three games in a season and was blown out nearly every week. It got to the point where I didn't even really expect to win but did keep a sliver of hope that we would.

Shortly after the season ended, I received my first visit from a college coach in the office of my head coach along with three other teammates. The coach from Willam Jewell gave his spiel on all the reasons why we should continue our athletic careers with his team. As previously stated, the idea of playing football in college was less than appetizing, but it had been the first time I realized colleges may be interested in having me on their team. The visits continued from other teams, Coach Pearson included, with mainly lackluster interest and participation on my part. At the time of the visits, I was in the middle of wrestling season, and I had put football on the backburner. With the finale of the wrestling season, I was once again able to focus on my football decision and career choice.

I had finally decided I was mainly interested in human anatomy and wanted to pursue a major related to that field. When I once again considered continuing to play football, I identified the pros and cons. I quickly surmised that many of the justifications I had previously listed as cons were experiences I missed when the season had initially finished. Whether it'd been the weight workouts I had to attend early in the morning, the extra conditioning the entire team had endured for the faults of a singular person, practicing in the freezing cold, or even the multiple losses my team and I had become accustomed to, they were all memories I deeply cherished. I began to remember why I enjoyed football in the first place. I loved being around all my teammates and going through our daily struggles together. I valued the physical and mental training I'd gained to be able to compete in the sport in the first place. It was all the little factors that made my involvement worthwhile and made every win, no matter how minimal, rewarding.

When I first visited Ottawa University, only four other schools were really in consideration: Kansas University, University of Kansas City-Missouri, Mid-America Nazarene, and Johnson County Community College. JCCC was the best financial option, but MNU and OU both offered me the opportunity to play football and get an education while not being too far from home. A considerable amount of my reasoning for not wanting to attend MNU was that it was less than ten minutes from where I lived and I wanted to be further away from home. KU and UMKC had mainly been considered if I went directly into the pre-med track.

As I toured the Ottawa campus, I was captivated by its smaller size, the rich history of the football team, a major that had an extensive support system/education, and the tight knit community that was described. When finally telling my parents that I planned to attend Ottawa, they were concerned that the tuition cost needed to be addressed. My older brother was just entering graduate school, and three more siblings are still waiting graduation after me—two in the next two years. I was soon informed that my GPA and ACT score qualified me to compete in the Top Scholars Competition and earn up to a full tuition scholarship which I immediately pursued. At that point, I no longer had any doubt concerning two major decisions of my life that had been so unclear at the onset of the senior year: football and where I would play.

First and foremost, I am looking to complete my education at Ottawa on time and with all the qualifications that can lead to acceptance in a graduate school for physical therapy. Now that I know what direction I'm headed in life, it excites me to see everything I can learn about the major that thoroughly intrigues me.

Second, I am prepared to play football for the coming years. It's always been a large part of my life and it brings me great joy to be able to continue playing into my young adult years. I know the history of the Ottawa Football team and plan to embrace the culture of my upperclassmen plus all of those who have played before me. I am eager to enhance my play and techniques, strengthen my football IQ, and most of all, help the team win.

Finally, I am ready to meet new people and make new connections while here in the Ottawa community. I want to be able to expand my horizons and experience new opportunities I've never exploited before. I await all the future sporting events I will attend where I will cheer on all the other Brave athletics. When COVID-19 is hopefully no longer a crucial part of our lives, I'll look forward to all the activities and festivities that regularly occur on campus. All in all, I am ready for the attractive opportunities that will be afforded me through my time at Ottawa University.

Yan Keuwo is a freshman from Olathe, Kansas. He is a member of the Braves football team and is majoring in exercise science. Yan expects to graduate in May of 2024. Following graduation, Yan plans to apply to graduate school.

ELI OWINGS

"Why did I choose Ottawa University?" Quite the question, isn't it? In my case, and the case of many top scholars, I think it is because of the opportunity.

When I received the letter telling me I had the opportunity to enter a contest to test my worthiness for a high achievers scholarship, I was dumbfounded. I knew colleges would desire my attendance because of my grades, but I certainly didn't think that possibly the most prestigious school in the state would actually offer me the chance to earn a full ride. The opportunity to study at such a place was almost incomprehensible for a small-town man like myself, yet the proof I had the chance was there before me.

The weeks leading up to the competition were high stress times for me. I knew I wasn't the best at speaking on the fly, and I had guessed (correctly) that was going to be an important part of the process. And the other competitors certainly gave me a run for my money! The stress in the days leading up to it, and actually participating, made it a wonder I could keep my composure.

A few weeks passed and then, there I was, January 27, 2020, in my Senior year of high school, 2:45, I got a text. It's from Ottawa with a number to call, and I know they're going to tell me whether or not I received the scholarship. My teacher excused me, I answered, it was Andy Otto, he told me I got it—a full ride. I then spent the rest of the phone call just thanking him and the university for giving me this great opportunity.

I had many plans to make my first year the best it could possibly be, things like joining the biology club, participating in as many school events as I could, and really getting into the spirit. I wanted to show my gratitude to the university in ways words could not!

And then *that* happened and threw everyone's plans into the garbage, stomping on them and then firing up the incinerator—just because it could as we all watched. I was angry and sad. I felt every emotion! This was the year I was to make memories I would cherish forever and it was all ruined. Just like that. Heck, my grandparents were going to take me on an eleven-day cruise around the Greek Islands. Neither words nor actions could describe my emotions when all that came to naught. My high school senior year? Crashed. My family's travel plans for the summer? Thrown out. That cruise? Apochairetismós (Greek for farewell)! I assumed my first year at college would be ruined, too.

Luckily, that last one didn't come to pass. The school's administration did everything it could to piece together a plan to allow students back for the fall semester. I always knew the transition from high school to college would be difficult, no matter where I attended, but going to a private school with plans made with the present circumstances in mind? It was even more difficult and strenuous than I anticipated.

Even though I gripe and moan like a child at the circumstances, I'm still grateful for the semester Ottawa was able to give me, and all of its students—even though it wasn't one any of us thought possible. And hey, it just makes me even more spirited when this pandemic eventually blows over. I'll be more enthusiastic at the events! Work even harder for the biology club that I forgot to join in all the chaos of the year! Look at more clubs to join, make and hang with friends—the whole shebang!

While I expected to end this semester with a big "hoorah," it obviously hasn't occurred in the manner I expected. This helped me see with clarity the things I take for granted, things like freely moving about, breathing in the fresh air, hanging out with friends, eating at restaurants—basically all facets of a normal life. When this is over, I am going to gather my friends and schedule hang outs with them. Maybe we can go golfing with one friend group and watch a movie or two with another? Take a group to supper at a restaurant? I don't know yet, and I'm excited to find out.

I had already committed myself to a biology degree with the end goal of becoming a physician's assistant, and this year has made me more certain than I thought possible! It awakened me to the fact that people have sicknesses that prevent normal interaction with the world lest it end with severe or lethal costs. These people need help. What kind of person would I be if I had the knowledge to make people's lives easier, more "normal," but did nothing with it? Every single mind working to unravel the secrets of these bugs and develop countermeasures increases the chances of a breakthrough where illnesses thought incurable suddenly have a means of allowing the person to live a normal life. That's my greatest dream, and every step is progress.

I also can't go without mentioning and offering my sincerest thanks to Ottawa's administration. I regret I can't name all of them because they deserve it for making a plan that allowed us back. I can mention a few staff here like Dr. Thomas Wiese, who worked with us on our labs in General Biology; President Wenyika, who offered a few motivational words when we passed each other; Andy Otto, who answered every question of mine that he could, and directed me to the people who could when he could not; and Dr. Zheng Chen, who was always willing to help guide me to the answer when I had a question on homework.

Ending this just wouldn't feel right without again extending my sincerest thanks to Ottawa University's staff, faculty, and administration. To every single one of you I say this: *Thank you*! I would also like to thank my friends who offered small reminders of how life once was, and how much better it will be when we take and learn from the lessons this tumultuous year has taught us.

Eli Owings is a freshman from Wellsville, Kansas. He is not currently a member of any extracurricular activities but plans on changing that in the coming year. Eli is majoring in biology and expects to graduate in May of 2024. After graduating, Eli plans to further his education to become a physician's assistant.

SECTION TWO

QUESTION TWO

"How have you changed during your time at Ottawa? What advice would you give to your first-year self if you could send yourself a brief note?"

Second-year scholars are coming into their own. Having for the most part found their bearings at the university and taken full control of the wheel, they are setting the course for the rest of their college careers and beyond. These students are in an exciting time in their lives, and it is both fun and heartwarming to hear about their own perception of this moment in their lives. These students have changed and grown, their introspective efforts are impressive, and their optimism is inspirational.

KAYLEN ASHLEY

If I had to explain how much I have changed since I arrived at Ottawa in my freshman year, I would liken myself to Heimlich, the caterpillar from *A Bug's Life*. I have transitioned from being chubby and anxious as I longed to be something I'm not, to actually becoming the thing I was longing to be. It has definitely been a long process, but I've ended up in the place in my life that I've wanted to be at since I was a little girl. There's still so much room for improvement, but I'm absolutely happy where I'm at, and I have Ottawa University to thank for that. Without this campus and the wonderful people on it, I would not be anything remotely close to the person I am today. From my friends to the professors who are helping me prepare for a career after I graduate, I have the most amazing support system, and I could not be more grateful.

Frankly, I sincerely doubt my younger self would even read a note I wrote to her because she always thought she was right about everything. However, if I had to write something on paper that would be crumpled and discarded immediately, it would be, "Hey Goofy, quit letting the fear of failure stop you from living your life, quit taking everything so seriously, and *let people help you*." Thankfully, over the course of the past year, I have somehow, someway managed to turn off the part of my brain that allowed me to worry about other people's perceptions of me. I definitely still want them to like me, but I no longer let it consume my life.

I have finally started to understand that no matter what I do, there will always be people who find some flaw with me—but that's on them. I was put on this Earth to do two things: eat an offensive amount of Sonic mozzarella sticks and live my life how I deem appropriate and necessary. I'm the only person in control of my life, and I'm the only one who should be pressuring myself to make decisions. Obviously, I'm not attempting to antagonize anyone purposely, and I still respect people and behave politely, but if someone has a bone to pick with me over nothing, then they're dealing with that on their own. I refuse to participate.

Not to toot my own horn, but I am much, much funnier than I was last year, and I'm also much happier. I now know that I can be goofy and have fun without compromising my integrity. My brother-in-law is one of the most professional people I know when it comes to his job. He does his work to the best of his ability all the time, and no one can doubt that he performs his duties spectacularly. He is very well-respected in the company where he works, as he should be because he's incredible.

Yet this same man got me a cake for my birthday that read, "HAP BIRDA." I have also walked in on him dancing with one of the cats in the kitchen. It took me much longer than it should have to realize that this is how it should be. I should be able to dork around and have fun and not be looked down upon just because I'm not stony-faced and quiet. Being happy shouldn't make people question if I can do my job, or if I am smart or anything like that. I laughed like twice a week last year. Now, I can't go more than five minutes without looking at one of my friends and giggling. Is it annoying for some people? I'm sure it is, but at least I'm enjoying my life and having a good time.

Letting people help me is still a struggle, but I'm pleased to say I've definitely gotten better at it. Academically, I used to hesitate asking people for help with my schoolwork even if I was struggling because I thought I was smart and I should know how to do it on my own. I used to get angry at myself if I couldn't figure out how to do something without assistance, and apparently had my head shoved so far up somewhere a head definitely shouldn't be that I couldn't ask for help. I thought that would be showing weakness, that it meant I wasn't as intelligent as I thought I was.

Thankfully, I got passed that when I realized one of my friends, who is one of the smartest people I have ever met in my whole life, had a tutor for one of the classes we were in together. They helped convince me that asking for help on an assignment didn't mean I was a failure; it just meant I needed a little push in the right direction. I discovered my academic strengths don't necessarily lie in creative thinking. If I am not taught how to do something in a detailed enough manner, I can't connect the dots between that and another concept very easily.

However, once I am taught something thoroughly, I understand it quickly and rarely forget how to do it. I haven't taken a physics class in years and could still find the velocity and displacement of a moving vehicle easily. Learning that some people are better in areas in which I'm weaker made things much easier for me, and I quit struggling through all my assignments alone. I've been a part of several study groups, and each one has helped me come away with an A in every class I've taken. I just had to let go of my pride a little bit and learn my own limitations.

In my personal life, it has definitely been a struggle to start accepting help as well. I was raised in a relatively unstable household where I grew up doing a lot of things for myself. My brother and sister were a fair amount older than I, so when they moved out, it left me alone with my mom and her boyfriend. Her boyfriend and I did not have the best relationship, and my mom refused to get in the middle of it, so I just sort of removed myself from the equation. I lived in the same house, but I rarely interacted with them outside of eating supper.

Because of this, I developed a sort of hyper independence where I no longer let people do things for me even if they wanted to. I got a job the day I turned 16, paid for everything I needed except for food, handled all of the things I needed to do to graduate from high school, paid for my own dual credit classes, started my own college fund, and I am currently still putting myself through school by working two jobs. Because of all this, I had convinced myself that I didn't need anyone to do anything for me, that I would be perfectly fine on my own. Obviously, I was totally, unarguably, ridiculously, woefully incorrect, but who admits that when they're 17? No one. If someone were to show me a 17-year-old that willingly admits to being incorrect, I would give them my entire life savings, which equates to about $5 and a half-eaten peanut butter and jelly sandwich—but that's beside the point.

During the second semester of my freshman year, my mom moved to Texas in an RV, leaving me in quite a predicament. I was still in Ottawa, about six hours away from my hometown and 13 hours from my mom, with $14 dollars in my bank account and half a tank of gas. There was no way I was making it to Texas on my own, and my mom had no money to send me, so I was essentially stuck in my dorm room with spring break quickly approaching. At the time, I was working as a practice manager for the women's basketball team under Bruce Tate and Brandon Bedell. Those men have both had a huge impact on my life, and I could never say enough good things about them. After hearing my situation, they offered to help me in any way they could, financially or otherwise, and while I was grateful and appreciative of them both, I couldn't bring myself to take their money.

Thankfully, my sister and her husband live an hour and a half from Ottawa, and they welcomed me into their house with open arms. They fed me and kept a roof over my head until I could get a job and start paying them back. My brother-in-law refused to let me pay them a dime until I had finished the semester and encouraged me to focus on my classes instead of worrying about them. I have no idea where I would be right now if it wasn't for them and for Ottawa. I can guarantee I definitely would not still be in college, and I will always be grateful to them for supporting me through this. Because of them and everything they've done for me, I'm still at Ottawa, double majoring in accounting and business economics, and maintaining a 4.0 GPA.

I'm the happiest and most successful I've ever been, and I'll always have my time at Ottawa to thank for that.

Kaylen Ashley is a sophomore from Oberlin, Kansas. She is double majoring in accounting and business economics and expects to graduate in December of 2022. Kaylen is currently undecided about her future career plans.

BRODY BURKHOLDER

"I can't change the direction of the wind, but I can adjust my sails to always reach my destination." - Jimmy Dean

Change is considered by many people, myself included, to be the only constant thing is life. Change is defined by *Webster's Dictionary* as "to make or become different." While on the surface this seems straightforward enough since we all pretty much know what the definition of change is, I believe that not many people know what it takes to truly make a change. It is commonplace in today's society for people to change their hair color, the way they dress, or the type of music they listen to. Fewer people can change their position in life to rise above the usual grind and better themselves. Fewer still can make an impact and change the world and the people around them. Perhaps fewest of all are the people who can change their mindset and the way they see the world around them—and in turn change the world around them by changing themselves.

This is what I have attempted to do in my time spent here at Ottawa. I say *attempted* not for lack of effort or education, but because change takes time. I change every day in the way I look at the people and places around me, and in the way I focus my energy. One of the biggest changes I have made since my arrival at Ottawa is the investment I have put into myself. This has occurred not only by getting older and out of the house as a young adult who is no longer a child, but also by playing a sport at the collegiate level and training intensely between 6 and 7 days a week. This has helped me understand that the body is a machine in the best and worst sense of the word. If I could reflect back and tell myself one thing relating to my physical performance, it would be to take care of my body as hard as I am going to work it. All the gains in the weight room and all the stamina built by pounding the pavement and the turf are meaningless if my legs are too sore to move in their full range of motion. All the dexterity and agility I have crafted running through field drills will never serve me if I tear an ACL or rotator cuff because I didn't take an extra five minutes to stretch.

Hindsight is always 20/20 and I would love to go back in time and tell myself to take better care of my mental health in addition to my physical health. I wish now more than ever I could tell myself to invest even more into my mental health than my physical health. It is easy to believe I am taking care of myself when I am seeing results. It is easy to convince myself I am mindful and productive when I am churning out multiple assignments a night and making the grades I need to make. Perhaps one of the most important sections of a letter to my previous self would be to reject the current societal view that mental health or mental soundness can be measured in production or what some people would call "success."

After starting for the lacrosse team, being elected president of Phi Delta Theta, starting an amazing internship for the Giveback Foundation, and participating in the Top Scholars Program on campus, I discovered that just because the things I align myself with may be productive, and I may see "results" doesn't mean they are productive and contributing to my well-being or nourishment. When I was most productive, I was my most miserable.

I wish I could go back and tell myself that busy work will always exist as long as the sun rises, but eventually the sun will set on my passions and youth. Although my energy is focused on fewer things these days, I have learned that the energy and focus I do expel towards the things in which I am involved is more focused and productive than ever before. Sometimes it is ok to do what is the best for me and release myself from other people's expectations of who I should be or what I should do. As the old adage goes, you can always retake a class, but you can never relive a party.

If I could tell my younger self one additional thing, it would be that taking studying seriously and retaining information are not only a must, but a privilege. As a child and throughout middle school and high school, I along with the most "gifted" or "advanced students" never had many issues with studying. I never was truly challenged by academic content until my last two years of high school, so I never really had to study or attempt to absorb information beyond a few obscure things that weren't in my immediate knowledge base.

Now I say this not out of pride or ego, but to help understand that until Ottawa, my strategy for absorbing important information was inadequate—to say the least. Much of the rhetoric and curriculum taught in high school and the lower levels doesn't result in demonstrating any fundamental understandings or grasp of topics. Neither do they encourage any free or abstract thinking in any capacity. So when most students first encounter the level of work required to stay afloat or even excel in college, it becomes as much a shock as it is an insult.

This sense of shock initially stems from worrying about academics and grades, which is something I had never had to do. The sense of insult came from years of rigid mainstream, standardized, testing-based education. The initial stress and worry of studying and trying to build useful information retention tactics are always the worst but as you adapt into the college mindset and delve deeper into classes and work, one breathes a sigh of relief, as we realize many other people are in the same boat. We learn that there is an army of spectacular professors and students who are more than willing to explain and assist us in the process of thinking creatively and abstractly.

What's more, the stress of academics is multiplied tenfold due to the fact that I (and all other scholars included in this collection) am a member of the Top Scholars Program, which hinges on academic performance rather than athletic performance like 96% of the general population of Ottawa University. However, my sense of insult came not from anything to do with academics or athletics. It did not come from Ottawa University or any professor, teammate, or fellow student. The insult did not emanate from Mrs. Grossman or Mr. Lanctot at Northridge High School, but rather at the public education system that had shaped my entire academic experience up to the time I arrived at Ottawa.

My sense of insult came from not ever being taught knowledge for the sake of being taught knowledge. In mainstream public education, value and worth are completely correlated with grade point average and "academic" achievement. The problem lies in the fact that public schools confuse academic achievement with digesting and regurgitating facts. This is where I wish I could go back and talk to my former self and help myself realize that knowledge is truly the one thing on this Earth that no one can take away from you. Knowledge—true knowledge and true understanding—is worth more than wealth and it is an absolute privilege to be taught and retain it.

Above all else, I would tell myself to be kind, not only to others and the environment and all things around me, but to myself as well. I have changed in incomprehensible ways, just as the world has around me has. I continue to change every second of every day, as does all humanity. No matter the number of hours I've spent with professors studying or lecturing, nothing can change the fact that at the end of the day, I am still me. No matter how many hours of manual work I have put into my body and muscles, it is still the same body I was born with. No matter how many unbreakable bonds and friendships and relationships I have forged, at the end of the night, I still go to bed with my own thoughts and conscience. At the end of the day above all else I must remember to be kind to myself.

Change is not immediate, but it is constant. If we did not change, we would not grow or make progress—and progress is not the only thing that matters. Change itself is the journey, and the glue that bonds all humans together. Therefore, be kind not only to others, the world, and all around you, but above all be kind to yourself. Change is not easy, so hang on—and keep being you.

Brody Burkholder is a sophomore from Middlebury, Indiana. He is a manager for the lacrosse team and a Top Scholar while also working as an intern with the Give Something Back Foundation in Ottawa. He is currently majoring in applied psychology and plans to work in community outreach in the future.

OTIS COSTLOW

During my time at Ottawa University my perceptions, comprehension, and attitude have changed dramatically—all for the better. These traits changed within me because I have made changes to my educational values and outlook of what I want to do with my degree from the University. The advice I would give to my first-year self if I could send myself a brief note would be to "stay true to yourself."

When I first arrived at Ottawa, my perception of the purpose of college was to get a degree and get out. As time has gone on, however, I noticed that the notion of my education to be a get-in get-out scenario is inescapably negligent. During my second year I knew I had to change how I approached the way I wanted to get my degree. Instead of continuing my approach of trying to obtain my degree as quickly as I could, I switched my perception to focus on my own edification.

I believe it is more significant to improve my intelligence and morals than to just have a lone goal of obtaining my degree. Essentially, I realize the point of college is to get a degree but there are more meaningful opportunities out there during one's time in college. To be able to find these opportunities, I must go out and identify them. I will not be able to improve myself and build my own portfolio if my time at college is wasted by not educating myself.

As my perceptions have changed throughout my second year, the biggest leap I took this year would be the comprehension of information presented to me. During my first year, the classes were at a higher level than I was expecting which made for a difficult transition from high school to college. My comprehension of the knowledge presented to me was low during my first year. At the time, my goal was just to pass the class and get by because the information presented was sometimes a bit too complex for me. However, I slowly improved my capabilities.

During my second year, I have become accustomed to the amount of information given in college courses. Now that I have become used to the difficulty and complexity of these courses, I now get the information and accurately process and dissect it and determine the purpose of the topics presented to me in my classes. Now that I am more used to the course schedule and the way college courses are taught, I am much more effective as I learn and comprehend the courses material my professors are teaching.

The most substantial change as I transitioned from my first to second year was in my attitude. As I began my freshman year, my attitude was poor. I was struggling with my classes and I remember thinking that I may not want to continue my college career. But as the year went on, I made it and my attitude started to improve. Now that I am in my second year at Ottawa University, my attitude has changed tremendously for the better.

Instead of thinking I could do the work, I instead tried to find ways that could help me accomplish what I wanted. Instead of sitting in class and concluding I would never be able to retain the information presented, I consulted with my professors about the information I did not understand to effectively determine whether I was properly understanding the information. The way I was able to change my attitude from my first to second year was to act without expecting results.

During my first year I was searching for optimal results. I wanted to go as fast as I could and finish school, but I realized that was an unrealistic and unnecessary goal. Since I am results-orientated, I ended up not doing everything I needed to do to effectively get the best education I can get. Now in my second year, I realize results are not everything. It is about the work that creates the result. Because results are not predetermined, they depend on the amount of work put into a project as to whether or not they yield good results. Now I do not expect results only to be disappointed when I do not get what I want. Rather than be disappointed, I can remember that I can do better and fix my bad attitude.

The transition from first to second year was something I was looking forward to because I knew there were unknowns during my first year that became knowns during my second year. Therefore, it would be easier to navigate the new obstacles of my second year using the knowledge I gained during my first year. Although there is nothing anyone can do to change the past, in my brief note to my younger self I would remind me to stay true to myself.

During college multiple obstacles and opportunities present themselves and as college students, we must often determine the best course of action with little or no help or input. Many people will influence or even try to determine which course of action is best for us. We must stay true to who we are to effectively make our college experience the best it can be. The best way to stay true to one's self is to first embrace our vulnerability and all aspects of our existence.

Let me make it more personal. The journey you are on is unique to each one of us so therefore you should not compare yourself with others. If you are struggling in a subject others think is easy, don't fret. Don't put yourself in situations where what you think you are not enough to meet the challenge, for your authenticity is always enough.

Next, understand your attitude towards adversity. As I mentioned earlier, my attitude needed to be improved in my first year. If you are facing adversity and you have a negative attitude, nothing positive is going to arise from the situation. Changing your attitude when faced with something you do not want can be life changing. Through a new attitude, you can instantly understand more thoroughly what you need to do to move forward despite the situation.

Finally, the most critical portion of staying true to yourself is doing what makes you happy when no one is looking. Throughout my first year of college, I found myself not paying attention to myself and what I wanted and instead relayed most of my focus into fulfilling my major and minor qualifications. During my first year my minor was psychology, and I was taking a few courses in those subjects. Throughout the year I did not enjoy my time in these classes, but I continued to take them. These classes were more of a fulfillment rather than something that I enjoyed.

Therefore, I changed my minor in my second year and now my class schedule is much more enticing and inviting than it was before. To create the life you want, you need to be the person you want to be instead of the one others expect you to be. Many people pursue status or success in order to be happy, but this approach is flawed. To be genuinely happy, you must be comfortable in your own skin and find out what makes you alone happy. Staying true to yourself is all about mastering how to live your life authentically rather than faking or forcing it. I would give my past self the advice to stay true to myself because at times last year I felt myself fading away. I was forcing myself into the monotony of going to class and then having nothing else on my mind but school problems. The most effective way of being the best college student possible is to be yourself.

In conclusion, from my first to second year I have changed in a multitude of ways. My perception has changed from getting my degree as fast as I can to focusing on my edification. Also, my apprehension of the material presented to me has drastically changed and I am now able to learn and retain the information to a greater degree than I previously could. Finally, my attitude adjustment of not letting the worst get the best of me and continuing to look ahead has given me a new approach to life and learning.

The advice that I would give my first-year self if I could send myself a brief note would be to stay true to yourself. You need to stay true to yourself because you will find that making decisions based on what will achieve your goals will help you achieve the life you want, and with each step your attitude will allow you to enjoy the process.

Otis Costlow is a sophomore from Overbrook, Kansas. He is majoring in business administration while minoring in psychology and expects to graduate in May of 2022. After graduation, Otis expects to further his education in the financial field.

JESSAMINE GREUTER

During my time as a student at Ottawa University, I have learned many important life lessons. I have also learned a lot about myself and what it means to be a successful and educated adult. Attending Ottawa has allowed me the space and time to change and reinvent myself. I have adapted my openness and work ethic, along with many other aspects of my life.

As a student, I have learned a lot about myself and the way I learn. I have discovered and perfected new and more efficient ways of studying. I have also learned the importance of taking time to study independently. In high school, I would rarely study alone. I would often study with friends and that often led to little work actually being done. Now I have learned that it is key for me and many others to study alone in order to be successful. I have found that working alone in the library is a great way for me to be both productive and be able to stay on task longer.

I have also learned the importance of asking questions and making connections with the teachers and staff. I have found that the staff here on campus whether they are in security, the cafeteria, or maintenance are extremely helpful and always excited to help us with anything we may need. The professors on the Ottawa campus are also always ready to help us with anything we need. They are always willing to reteach or explain concepts in a way that we better understand. I have found that visiting them during office hours and staying connected with the professors is key to succeeding here at Ottawa.

If I were able to write a letter to my first-year self, I would include three important lessons I learned during the past two years.

First, I would tell myself to learn to relax more and go with the flow. Life is full of challenges and surprises. I have to learn to adapt easily to change and take things as they come. It's important to not spend all of my time stressing about the future. I never know what is going to happen in the next hour let alone the next year. After COVID hit in 2020, everyone had to move back home and switch to online learning. For many students, including myself, learning how to adapt to change was vital during this time. Overnight I had to move home and learn how to manage doing all of my assignments and activities online.

This taught me that worrying about the future and stressing about what is going to happen next is irrational. It is better to focus on what is happening now rather than worrying about what will happen later on. I wouldn't say that I shouldn't have a plan. It is always better to be prepared, however, and being able to adapt and change that plan when needed is vital. Not all change is a bad thing. For example, new roommates, classes, and friends are small changes in my life can make a huge difference.

Second, I would tell my first-year self that it is important to make connections with the amazing staff on campus as soon as possible. The staff on campus are always helpful and happy to help us with whatever it is we need. The maintenance and security men are always available to help us if we get locked out or if something needs to be fixed in the dorms. The professors and staff in administration are always eager to help us with whatever we need. The Campus Ministries is also a great on campus organization that is always ready to help students. It is also important to get to know the staff in the health office and the counseling center. The campus provides excellent physical and mental health services for students. If we ever feel sick or unwell Nurse Martha is the one to go to. She is always there eager to help us feel better.

Lastly, I would tell myself to get involved. There are tons of activities on campus that are incredibly fun if we are simply willing to go out and try new things. There are tons of fun clubs that hold events and fun activities on campus. There are fantastic musical programs such as choir, band, pep-band, and theater. Even if we are not interested in getting involved in a club or organization going out and supporting the many Ottawa University sports teams is a great way to get involved in campus life. There are always games happening on or around campus. Even though it can be intimidating, attending sporting events and campus life activities are always a great idea and fun way to get to know people on campus.

Overall, I would tell my freshman self to simply enjoy it. If I thought the years of high school flew by, I don't think I have seen anything yet. There are tons of activities and things to do on campus. There are hundreds of amazing people to get to know and learn from. I should try to enjoy every minute of it. Whether studying, eating with friends, playing in the pep-band, taking a quick nap before class, or just walking around campus, take the time to enjoy it. The time here on campus flies by, because time flies when you're having fun.

Jessamine Greuter is a sophomore from Topeka, Kansas. Jessa is majoring in secondary education English with a minor in history and expects to graduate in May of 2023. After graduating, she plans to teach in the Topeka Public School System.

COLLIN HANSON

"Life is growth. If we stop growing technically, and spiritually, we are as good as dead" (Unknown).

My thinking as a freshman was that I was attending Ottawa University for the sole purpose of pursuing a career and challenging myself athletically. After the first semester, I began to realize just how much I was learning that was unrelated to my studies and athletics. While I was in fact acquiring information at a fast pace and growing in my education, I was also growing into a person of tremendous responsibility and faith. I was gaining virtues that I had never even dreamed of, and they have shaped me into the person I am today.

Growing up, I learned responsibility from my parents and they played a crucial role by pouring into me in order to help shape me into a responsible adult with excellent morals. However, I came to college and immediately was forced to learn responsibility on a whole new level. Suddenly, my parents weren't there to remind me to study. They weren't there to provide me with delicious meals. They certainly weren't there when my car broke down on the side of a major highway. All of these things were now up to me to figure out, and with everything on the line, I had to make decisions that could be difficult.

Living on my own at Ottawa University, I have quickly realized that my decisions have consequences. Sometimes they are positive, but in other instances, they are negative and often challenging. It is because of these negative consequences that I now think twice before making decisions and weigh the possible outcomes. Overall, I have gained a lot of responsibility in living on my own, and Ottawa University has certainly played a tremendous role in my growth.

As a second-year junior, I made another decision that would change my life forever. I applied to be a resident assistant in Bennett Hall. The task came with plenty of challenges but taught me more about life than just about anything else. As an RA I was given the task of being an on-campus resource for any resident who needed it. The responsibilities of an RA go so far beyond the stereotype of enforcing dormitory rules, and I did not know this when I applied. It became my responsibility to create relationships with all of my residents, document anything unusual, creatively plan programs designed to encourage social, intellectual, spiritual, and physical experiences.

In addition I worked at the desk, and had the opportunity to be in charge of 150 students safety and well-being at times. Unfortunately, I am unable to go into detail about some of my experiences, but certainly there were extremely challenging times as an RA when I was under great stress and did not know what to do. It was this job that has grown me into the person I am today. It has taught me the importance of relationships in college and making connections with people. I have long-standing relationships with some of my residents I would never have gained if I was not an RA. The training that Ottawa University provided me is something I will be able to use for a lifetime. My creativity, ingenuity, organization, communication skills, and so much more have improved ten-fold since becoming a resident assistant. In the end, being an RA gave me plenty of knowledge and skills I will continue to use for years to come.

There were multiple organizations and clubs I have been involved with during my time at Ottawa University. I am presently involved in the Fellowship of Christian Athletes and serve on the leadership team, as well as the Executive Philanthropy Chair for the Phi Delta Theta Fraternity on campus. I am in the Biology Club, and I also tutor for biology and writing. In general, I am quite busy all the time, but these clubs and organizations have grown me as a person greatly.

Being a leader for Fellowship of Christian Athletes has given me the opportunity to share the Bible as well as personal experiences with many students at Ottawa university. It has improved my speaking skills and confidence more than any speech class could ever do. Being student led, it has also given me great opportunities to make decisions for the club. In addition to all of this, I lead worship for FCA, which includes playing the guitar and singing. It is a time of great spiritual growth for me and anyone else in attendance.

As far as the Fraternity goes, I was first the Warden, which is an executive position tasked with keeping order in meetings, and monitoring behavior and academic performance within the fraternity. It gave me more administrative and relational skills, and so much more. I then became the philanthropy executive chair which means I am the leader in raising money for various charitable causes. It has taught me the importance of giving back to the community and being a person who cares for more than just myself. All of these clubs and organizations have had amazing impacts on my life, and Ottawa university does an extraordinary job in sponsoring them.

Another supremely influential factor in my personal growth at Ottawa University is my internship with Pastor Dakota Smith of Ottawa

Bible Church. My faith and spiritual life have always been a substantial part of my life but taking on an internship increased my growth in that area more than I could have dreamed possible. Essentially, my role as an intern consists of meeting with Pastor Dakota as well as two other interns and growing together in faith. More importantly, we were able to start a college ministry that meets off of campus where we provide excellent food, worship, and a message. My role as an intern is to lead to worship through playing guitar and singing, preparing slides, and choosing worship songs. In addition, I have been able to give my testimony and share my faith with others.

The internship has given me more strength and confidence in my faith and has shown me the importance of building long-lasting relationships with people who share the same beliefs with me. This internship has taught me to see the good in the world and remain optimistic in circumstances that may appear bleak. I have learned to love others unconditionally and respect people no matter what their beliefs, and it has truly changed my life in a positive way. In the end this internship has taught me so much about life and has given me many reasons to enjoy life more.

Truly, college is an amazing time of life. It is a time when change is constantly taking place in one's life, and we are forced to either take advantage of it or be beaten down by it. While attending Ottawa University, my life has been altered greatly from the first day I stepped on campus. I was never exactly a shy person, but when I first came to Ottawa, I certainly was nervous. However, now that has all changed. I live life excited for each day and look forward to what the day brings me.

My creativity has improved greatly to the point that my mind is constantly full of fresh new ideas that I am eager to tell people about. Study time is no longer a burden, but rather a time of peace and tranquility in which I am able to be thankful for the wonderful opportunities God has given me through Ottawa University. I have plenty of outstanding friends I never would have met had I not come to college, and I know with absolute certainty that many of them will be lifelong friends. Since that first day on campus, I am truly alive and seeing the world for what it is, but more importantly what it could be.

The idea behind going to Ottawa University is to "prepare for a life of significance." Before coming to Ottawa, I did not have a clue of what that looked like, but looking back now, it is much simpler than I was making it out to be. I feel like I have so much purpose in life, and I always want to bring the best out of myself and others. To say my life has improved would be a gross understatement. The world I live in may not be the same as it was when I first stepped foot on campus, but that simply means I have grown, and am going to have more opportunities to do so. I am at the point in college where I can truly say I am not just going through the motions and doing enough to get by. Rather, I am working hard in anticipation of the time when I am living a life of significance. I am not just simply living. I am thriving.

Collin Hanson is a junior from Ottawa, Kansas. He is a member of the men's golf team, leader of FCA, and executive philanthropy chair of the Phi Delta Theta Fraternity. Collin is majoring in biology and minoring in chemistry (pre-med). He plans to graduate in May of 2022 and attend the Kansas University School of Medicine.

LAWSON MEDLEN

College is a serious, life-changing event. Those reading this statement who have attended college will certainly agree. Even transitioning from high-school life to adulthood is huge. My first year of college at Ottawa University has seriously changed who I am as a person. I had great fun doing this, but in a sense, I have also matured a lot. I've learned to apply myself more to a college and adult setting. From getting involved in clubs to working my tail off in classes, I feel I've started to develop a great work ethic for my future career. Overall, there is a lot that has changed since my initial steps into campus life.

My first significant change is my sociability. In high school, I was a pretty social person, but I had been around those people my entire life. When I got to college, it was all back to step one: How to I make friends again? To do this, I decided I needed to apply myself as much as possible. I joined the tech club, played tennis, played in jazz band and wind ensemble, joined FCA, and even today I'm a resident assistant and involved in a college ministry. All of these activities, along with my classes, have helped me build friendships with an entirely different crowd than I was used to. I've become a much more sociable person and can connect with complete strangers at ease.

Something crazy I realized about my first-year struggles was that several other students were probably going through the same thing. I wanted to help incoming students as much as I could. I remembered how when I had a difficult time coming out of my room, my resident assistant always found a way to talk to me. I decided to apply and become a resident assistant for my second year at Ottawa University. The training required for this job gave me skills that will help me for the rest of my life. I now know how to handle difficult situations professionally and how to connect with other people and get them help when need be. I also had to learn how to manage my time better than I had. Time management is required for anyone who is busy at college. I can now organize my hectic schedule and prioritize all immediate tasks that need to be done.

I've also grown spiritually since I've joined Ottawa University. Taking my required Gospels course, along with personal growth and Development days (PGDs) has really helped me connect with God and be at peace. I wrote a ten-page paper in Gospels class about what else? The Gospels! In this paper, I felt that I knew so much more as a Christian than a year beforehand. I really want Ottawa to keep this program required for students that come here. I understand that not all students that come here are Christian, but this is a private school. I also feel that there are a lot of people in the world who haven't even really heard the story of the Gospels.

With a stronger connection to my religion, I was encouraged to go to church more, join our college ministry, and attend FCA regularly. I now find peace whenever there is worry, and trust in my heart that God is in control of all aspects in my life—even the bad ones. Whatever may happen in my future years, I understand God's will and will always surrender to it. I now hope to help others in the future to connect more with God and facilitate healing for those who may need it. I also hope to worship God more through my music in the future when I find more time to practice my instruments.

The last part of my freshman year during which I grew the most is when COVID-19 sent us all home. Although this isn't an OU exclusive experience, it was an experience I had while still in classes. Getting sent home to online classes, I learned how to adjust to quickly changing conditions and scenarios that can be so stressful. Even though it was a stressful and different experience, I still got to connect a little with my professors and other students online. I really enjoyed having the professors I did as they kept us involved as much as they could. I also still got to connect with my friends online.

To deal with any hurt feelings or disappointment I had at the time, I decided to cope in a healthy way. Living in the country by a *beautiful* trail near my home, I constantly ran and road my bike. I exercised a lot to help improve my mood. I buckled down and decided to improve myself as much as possible, and I believe this is where I grew the most in my freshman year. I had lost my freshman tennis season into which I had devoted a stupendous amount of effort and time. It only felt good to stay in shape. I also improved my mood by working a very fun job at the Pomona Lake Marina. After all this healthy coping, I ended up having one of the best spring/summers of my life. I enjoyed the environment, enjoyed my job, and enjoyed my lifestyle. This is the biggest part of my freshman year, and maybe even my life, where I have grown into an independent, happy person.

There is so much advice I could give my former self if I could. I could think of ten things off the top of my head I would tell myself *not* to do. The main thing I think I would tell myself is this one crucial thing: "You're not alone, and you need to remember that there is nothing wrong with you. There is nothing you should change about yourself for others." I really struggled for a while with being alone my first year. I did take steps to help fix that, and become more social like I said earlier, but that doesn't mean I no longer struggled with the issue. I had been around people who knew me my whole life, and typically people talked to me thinking, "This is Lawson, the silly, nice guy."

When I got to college, I probably looked at me like "This is Lawson, the giant scary teddy bear." This made it a little more difficult to socialize with others around me who didn't know I probably couldn't hurt a fly. I needed to let myself know that there wasn't anything wrong with me, that I just need to be patient and keep working hard. I needed to give myself time to adjust to college instead of freaking out and thinking poorly of myself. It took the friends I did happen to make and a lot of personal goals to get over this mentality.

Another thing I would also tell myself is to never give up on anything I love. I feel that even though I still worked hard on myself, I kind of gave up tennis and music when situations got complicated and difficult to improve. I really should have tried to work harder to practice and enjoy these talents I had come to love. To this day, I still miss the tennis team and playing in a sport. I also miss involving myself more in our music programs, but because of some of the COVID-19 restrictions at hand, I decided it would be best to focus on other things. I will one day hopefully resume these activities I've loved for so long, but right now I've decided to focus on my future.

Ottawa University is still preparing me and will always prepare me for a life of significance. I've enjoyed my time at OU so far, even though some aspects have had negative downturns. Ottawa has still kept us open the 2020-21 school year and I'm truly thankful for that. They have taken the precautions they need to ensure that our students can still come and have a college experience. I will forever remember the 2019-2020 school year because it has been one of the most diverse years of my life. It's been fun, happy, sad, boring, heart breaking, uplifting, and unique.

Most of all, this last year has been about growth. Of all the topics I could've been tasked with writing over. I think growth was the best subject that could have been given. There are two ways you can look at the 2019-2020 school year: This year has been the biggest disaster of our lives, and we should always turn away from and never think about 2020; or, we can look at it that during this year we have learned to adjust to changing conditions. We have grown into stronger versions of ourselves, and we've learned to love and appreciate what we have.

Everyone deserves to be happy, and I truly believe that people can only find happiness in themselves. We must form our own lives with our own mindsets. This is how we will grow as people.

Lawson Medlen is a sophomore from Ottawa, Kansas. He is a member of the Ottawa Reslife staff, FCA, Tech Club, Abide (college ministry), and the Federalism, Freedom, and Flourishing Book Club. Lawson is majoring in business economics and accounting with a concentration in finance, and expects to graduate in May of 2023. Following graduation, Lawson plans to apply to graduate school.

DERRIANE MORRISON

I began my journey to Ottawa University in December of my senior year of high school. Before then, I was sure I was going to wrestle at a school in Missouri but my parents advised me to keep my options open. Thankfully, my coach sent my film and information to different schools that had a women's wrestling team. Doing that gave me a better chance at continuing my passion for wrestling at a higher level. The process of choosing a school to attend was not the easiest, but luckily it all worked out in the end.

One day, in the middle of wrestling practice, I received a phone call from the head wrestling coach in Ottawa. I have talked to many coaches across the country, but something about the coaches here was different. They talked to me as if I was already a member of their team and I had not even applied to the school yet. Later that day, I was set up to apply the following month and scheduled a visit in March.

Even though I ended up applying to OU in January, I was still a little skeptical about attending Ottawa. The other school I had in mind had been looking at me to wrestle for them since my freshman year of high school. They were also giving me a wrestling and academic scholarship to come to their school. By the middle of February, I was accepted into Ottawa University, and all that was left for me to do was to choose which institution I wanted to attend. Luckily, I received an email from Ottawa discussing that they were interested in me for the school's scholar's program.

While I knew the program could be a great opportunity for me, I became hesitant to submit my application. I was not sure if I would even get accepted into the program let alone win any of the scholarships, but yet again my parents pushed me to try anyway. I can honestly say that my family has been my support system throughout the entire process because later that month I got a call that I was accepted. I was also informed that the competition would be held in March which could not have worked out more perfectly.

My original time to visit was the week of my spring break and the scholar's competition was only two days before I was scheduled to arrive. At this time, things remarkably started to come together towards the end of my senior year. I finished my four-year-long journey of being a wrestler in high school and was ready to continue at a college level.

After a 12-hour drive from Houston, Texas to Ottawa, Kansas, the entire wrestling team met me and my family for dinner at Smoked Creations. I had never felt more welcomed by a group of people. Not only did the restaurant have great food, the team brought another recruit who was also interested in wrestling. It was nice to know I was not alone in the process of wanting to be an athlete in college. We came from similar backgrounds and she has become my best friend and sister in college.

The scholar's competition proceeded the next day and I can honestly say that I was extremely nervous. While the process seemed to last forever, I received the results the following Monday after my tour. I could not have been prouder of myself for being the next presidential scholarship recipient. Teary-eyed phone calls were made to many of my family members and my coach the entire week. Winning the competition was my assurance that Ottawa is where I was supposed to be.

However, by the time I came home, the entire world seemed to be in question. The coronavirus was turning into a pandemic and millions of people had suffered because of it. I knew that I still wanted to attend Ottawa, but I was unsure of what my first year of college would look like. Thankfully, the staff at Ottawa came together and created a way for students to go to school in person while keeping six feet apart. While that is not the ideal situation, it is better than nothing. Attending college during a pandemic is most definitely an experience I will never forget.

This coming year, I am looking forward to more experiences and new memories. Living in Texas is completely different from living in Kansas, so I have had to learn and adapt to the new environment, especially the weather. Coming from a large city like Houston, Ottawa is a bit of an adjustment. My high school consisted of around 4,000 students, while the university has less than 800 students on campus. Ottawa University is its own little community where everyone pretty much knows everyone, which is something I am not yet accustomed to.

This past semester has already been such a learning experience for me. While it was not perfect, I met some of the most amazing people who I can now call my family. Being away from home has allowed me to understand myself and learn the kinds of people I want to surround myself with. I also look forward to understanding more about what it takes to become a physical therapist. The classes I took last semester have already opened my eyes to the many opportunities I will have after graduating from Ottawa, whether that is to continue wrestling at a higher level or receive my doctorate in physical therapy.

While my goals may not seem to be the easiest to achieve, things worth doing are often difficult. Fortunately, many students here at Ottawa have similar goals in education so I have never felt out of place when preparing for classes or discussing the plans I have for the future. Therefore, I am extremely grateful for everyone involved in the process and cannot wait to see the outcome of my first year in college.

Derriane Morrison is a freshman from Houston, Texas. She is a member of the women's wrestling team and Campus Activities Board. Derriane is majoring in exercise science and expects to graduate in May of 2024. Following graduation, she plans to attend graduate school to pursue a career in physical therapy.

SECTION THREE

QUESTION THREE
"What, in your opinion, is the real purpose of a liberal arts education? What excites you most about your future?"

People often tout the benefits of a liberal arts education. When questioned further, these same people often reveal they don't have a firm grasp on what comprises such an education or what special features render it a particularly valuable education and why.

Our third-year scholars, on the other hand, are in the trenches, fighting to acquire that liberal education. That's the reason we ask them, having completed more than half of their college education, to reflect on the value of what they are receiving. It is instructive to hear from them concerning what they value about their education and what they plan to do with the investment they have made. I'm glad to say our students have planned well, understand the value of their education, and are prepared to make the most of the opportunities coming their way. I'm sure you'll agree.

TRENTON BARROWS

Liberal arts education has been a revered resource for thousands of years because it creates well-rounded individuals who excel at problem solving and communication skills with a broad understanding of many subjects. This makes them adaptable to a rapidly evolving work and cultural environment. Having a degree of this nature prepares the holder to work in a variety of different sectors and can be contoured to meet the demands and opportunities of a wide range of available jobs.

This education also helps introduce students to career pathways they may not have originally considered or found interesting while they were in the middle of their studies. Also, employers in the modern workforce are aware of the transferable skills taught to liberal art students, which qualifies them to obtain careers after graduation that have potential for growth. This paper will analyze the history of liberal arts, how it has adapted to today's society, and the benefits of obtaining this degree—along with my personal experience of attending a liberal arts college.

Beginning around the time of ancient Greek civilization, liberal arts was seen as the ultimate mark of an educated person. Historically there were seven major topics taught in this form of education which were divided into two groups known as the trivium and quadrivium. Known as the "Father of Liberal Arts," famous Greek philosopher Aristotle placed the utmost importance on the first three subjects: grammar, rhetoric, and logic (the trivium). He believed that by obtaining knowledge and mastering these topics, students would be prepared for real-world problem solving with the commensurate communication skills required enabling members of society to participate in civil duties such as debate and jury and court participation.

Traditionally, members of the liberal arts community would learn the trivium first so they could convey their messages clearly and with conviction, and then learn the next four subjects of arithmetic, geometry, music, and astrology (the quadrivium). These subjects were used to prepare students for more serious study of theories and philosophy and were considered much more difficult than the original three studies. While these studies are divided into two different groups, the purpose of learning and utilizing both the social and physical sciences is that they are complementary in nature since the student must not only understand the material they are researching but must also present their findings and disburse that expertise among other individuals in a society.

In modern day liberal arts, a much broader spectrum of studies is offered, along with majors allowing students to obtain a liberal arts degree while focusing on a specific area of study that intrigues them in the United States. Unlike the historical arrangement of liberal art studies, it now generally encompasses four main topics of study with slight variation depending on the specific institution. First is humanities, considered to be the modern trivium, which includes art, speech, theater, music, foreign language, and literature. Next are the natural, formal, and social sciences. Social sciences include the studies of history, psychology, politics, economics, and business informatics. Classes like mathematics, logistics, and statistics fall under the formal science category, while classes such as astrology, biology, chemistry and geology are classified as natural sciences. While these four classifications exist, it remains true that a well-rounded education is to be expected from a liberal arts institution.

At Ottawa, students are required to fulfill "breadth areas" before continuing with their decided major—a term that is given to courses within specific schools in the university. The purpose of this setup is so students enroll in classes they would never take within their major in order to give them a diversity of exposure, to help them achieve a mastery of a wide range of transferable skills, and possibly to spark interest in a new career path they previously hadn't foreseen. Once a student decides on their major, they are then admitted into that school where they will continue to take more advanced courses in that area of study while still fulfilling all of the breadth area requirements. This form of liberal art education differs from the schooling received at other institutions in the sense that most other colleges follow a strict research-based curriculum on a specific subject.

Compared to state-funded universities, liberal art institutions are viewed as small schools that don't have access to the same resources as their larger counterparts. The focus on innovative research is much higher in big universities, and education tends to be much cheaper with their large enrollment rates. General facilities at universities are more up-to-date and technologically advanced, which is appealing to the vast majority of students who enroll in higher education. Due to these factors, it is often believed that students at nationally recognized schools have better understanding of specific material and mastery within their specified major coupled with experience using the most current business practices. It is also notable that larger colleges have more recognition among the workforce and therefore can carry a certain reputation based on the name alone. Their large base of pubic awareness and alumni helps students at large universities make connections for job opportunities as well.

Despite these facts, it is essential to note that the first part of a liberal arts education is the trivium, which is advanced social and communication skills. The emphasis these larger institutions place on technical skills and research advancements often neglect the importance of vital skills for real world application. While lower enrollment does raise the price of the education at private schools, it lowers the teacher-to-student ratio in a classroom which allows for more personalized learning and more fruitful classroom discussion where students can interact with each other. The lower numbers of students also allows a stronger bond between the students and faculty, which can be beneficial towards expanding a student's opportunities in and out of the university while improving a student's ability to interact with superiors.

Professors and administration are more likely to be flexible with their students in this setting, given that it is communicated clearly with advanced notice. This more easily allows the students to fill their day with extracurricular activities such as sports, community service, school-regulated clubs, and internships. Due to this relationship, it tends to be easier for liberal arts students to obtain letters of recommendations for graduate programs. Students attending a liberal arts college also have greater access to undergraduate research opportunities, while most state-funded colleges offer this to their graduate schools, making it a highly competitive and scarce commodity. While the students at large universities have a higher quantity of connections, the quality of connections at liberal art colleges tends to be greater which can help students land internships and job opportunities. What I am most excited about for my future is to utilize the knowledge I am obtaining at Ottawa and see what all I am capable of achieving with a Liberal Arts degree.

Throughout high school, like most students, I had no intention of attending a private university and was set on applying to large state schools such as Kansas University or the University of Alabama. I believed this was not only in my best interests because it was much cheaper, but also because the connections with so many alumni could help me achieve my future goals. My thoughts on what exactly I wanted to study while in school changed quickly, however, starting with me wanting to major in biology and possibly attend medical school through Kansas University. It wasn't until Ottawa offered me the chance to play a sport that I made a campus visit and ultimately settled on my decision to come to Ottawa. The people, professors, and administration I had met while on my visit played a big role in my feeling comfortable with my decision, even if I was unsure what the school could offer me for future ventures.

I was a business administration major in my freshman year with a minor in biology because I thought I wanted to open my own medical practice after college. As I took more classes, the liberal arts education had placed me into a plethora of classes I don't think I would have come into contact with if it wasn't for the diverse education provided at such a college like Ottawa. I still didn't quite understand the importance of liberal arts education, and throughout my first two years struggled with the justification of paying for this degree—nearly dropped out a few times. If it wasn't for my teammates and some of the professors I had met within those crucial years, I most likely would not be at Ottawa any longer.

Nonetheless, I decided to push aside my negative thoughts and continue with the path I had chosen. While continuing with my schooling, I had taken more classes in the school of business and found a love for marketing and a natural ability to perform well in accounting. While I wasn't quite fond of my accounting classes my professor, Lyn Wagner, had a large influence in my life. As previously mentioned, the smaller teacher-to-student ratio that only exists in a liberal arts college allows for students to form bonds with the faculty, which can assist the students in receiving professional guidance on how to achieve their goals. Lyn became my advisor after I had become an upperclassman and would schedule meetings with me to talk about what I wanted to do after graduation.

Upon sharing that I eventually would like to open my own business, she directed me toward classes she believed would help me run a business efficiently and effectively. Other professors in my classes allowed students to take on specialized roles that gave them a unique experience and opportunity to apply their own skill set rather than a set course. Once I realized the value a liberal arts school provides me, I felt as if I had dodged a bullet by not attending a large state university. With the adversity that I faced along the way, I believe Ottawa has already prepared me for a life of significance.

Once I receive my bachelor's degree, I would like to continue my education through Ottawa and receive my master's degree in business. Many of my teammates chose this path and have urged me to follow in their footsteps, expressing their belief that it is beneficial.

After that is taken care of, I would like to use my marketing degree to get a job in a large city since I have learned that is where opportunities for growth present themselves more frequently. I intend to use this experience not only to earn money but also to obtain knowledge of the industry as a whole, and then utilize that knowledge and apply it to my future business endeavors.

Once I have gained the experience and capital to achieve my ultimate goal of running a business, I would like to return to Kansas where I will operate my business in order to give back to the community I grew up in, along with the university that prepared me for this adventure. I am baffled that I previously had no intention of considering a school like Ottawa and am deeply grateful how everything fell into place, allowing me to find a purposeful and meaningful path to follow.

Trenton Barrows is a junior from Overland Park, Kansas. He is a captain of Ottawa men's lacrosse team and a Provost Scholar. Trenton is majoring in accounting and minoring in marketing and expects to graduate May of 2022. Following graduation, he plans to join the workforce to gain experience for future business ventures.

ANGEL GARRETT

Ottawa University has a motto visible under the university seal on every platform: Prepare for a life of significance. As a junior at Ottawa, I can attest to the fact that the university does just that. Ottawa has a liberal-arts-centered education, which provides the students with a well-rounded outlook on life. A liberal arts education is one that insists all students take classes outside of their chosen major.

College is about determining what you plan to do with your future. Some people come into college with a good idea of their future plans, while some have no idea at all—and some people change their original ideas multiple times. In my opinion, a liberal arts education helps to ease some of the pressure of trying to find out what you want to do on your own. This is because the liberal arts student is required to take courses in the fine arts, social sciences, natural sciences, and communications fields along with the courses required for one's major. Because we are required to take a greater selection of classes than other schools, students are able to explore multiple areas of study.

While exploring these other areas, it is not uncommon for some people to realize that what they originally thought they wanted to do is actually not something they are passionate about. Life is all about choices, and as we grow up, we have a lot of those choices to make, but we are told that we have time to make them. When we get to high school, the idea of making choices starts to get more difficult and pressing because once we graduate, we are about to start paying a lot of money for the next level of education and want to ensure that we are not wasting the opportunity—or the money.

When we are actually in college, time has almost run out to decide what we want to do in life, and a lot of people feel trapped in the major in which they started. I feel like having a liberal arts education dissipates a lot of that stress because with a liberal arts education, we do not really have to know what we want to do yet because we get to take classes in every area.

Not only does it relieve the stress of feeling as though we have to know what we want to do as soon as we get to college, but it creates a new stress in that a liberal arts education forces us out of our comfort zone. This is especially true at Ottawa because we are a faith-centered university and a course *The Gospels* is required for all students to take for a semester. That being said, not all students who attend the university are religious, so this required class is a prime example of being pushed out of one's comfort zone through a liberal arts education.

Along with forcing the students out of their comfort zone, a liberal arts education also provides them with a more well-rounded education. Having classes in multiple areas of life allows for their outlook on life to be broader and perhaps even forces them to be more open-minded. This is especially true when moving into a profession. A liberal arts education could set them above others that are also going for the same job simply because it broadens their capabilities and intellect.

This form of degree allows people to look at a specific profession differently. For example, a student could be an accountant with a liberal arts degree and because of that, they are forced to have a more creative approach to learning, which is much more appealing to employers and potential clients. A liberal arts degree also improves communication in the sense that there is a better understanding of all aspects of life instead of one singular outlook. This means that it would be easier to talk to people because the liberal arts graduate is able to understand not only a mathematician, but also an artist or a scientist. This does not mean that a graduate will know all the career-specific vocabulary others use, but they should have a general understanding of the situation being discussed which will allow for better communication rather than a binary understanding of only the student's profession or area of expertise.

Along with effective communication comes the ability to collaborate and adapt to change. It is easier to collaborate with someone who has a basic understanding of multiple disciplines than with someone who may see their specific discipline as the most important. In the world in which we live, there is a lot of change every single day. Change is something everyone has to be able to work with, but those with a liberal arts education will have a better grasp on how to adapt to change due to the fact that they have a well-rounded and comprehensive look at life and work in general.

From the perspective of an employer, a liberal arts education may show a desire to continue learning rather than just completing a specific degree. This means that rather than having tunnel vision where one specific job or career is concerned, an employer may see someone with a liberal arts education as a person who is willing to do a job similar to the one for which they applied—one that is perhaps slightly different and more challenging. Someone with a liberal arts education is more likely to be a leader in their profession because of their vast understanding of multiple areas and their ability to think critically as well as problem solve and consider multiple points of view.

College is all about finding out what we want to do in life and pursuing that future goal through education. When it comes to my future, I have some pretty ambitious plans. While growing up, just like any other child, I constantly changed my idea of what I wanted to do in life, but there was always one constant in that for me. That constant was the desire to help others. It was never about money to me, but rather about the little voice that was constantly in the back of my head telling me I needed to make a difference in the world.

Now, when most people think about helping others, they think of first responders or teachers or therapists, but I took a different and slightly unconventional approach to what it meant to help others. Of course, I originally planned on being a veterinarian, as some children do, and then a teacher, then even a writer, but all that changed when I took anatomy and physiology in high school. I had always hated science—not disliked, *strongly* hated. Once I took anatomy, however, that view started to change.

I realized then I didn't hate science, I just preferred science I could see and touch, rather than learning about molecules that aren't visible to the naked eye or elements I could not touch without burning off skin. The idea of the body and how it worked were fascinating to me, and after that class, I knew science was something I wanted to pursue in life. Although I enjoyed anatomy and physiology, in no way, shape, or form did I have *any* desire to be a doctor. In my opinion, that was just too much pressure. I didn't like the idea of having someone else's life in my hands.

So, I looked at the other end of that: What if I helped people who were no longer living? And that is when I realized that I wanted to do forensic science. Working in a forensic lab meant I could get the best of both worlds: science and helping others. I would be able to run biological tests off collected evidence and eventually trace the results back to the perpetrator of a crime (hopefully).

When it comes to working in a forensic science laboratory, there are multiple areas of expertise: biology/DNA, trace evidence, toxicology, latent prints, crime scene investigation/collection, firearms, and other areas. The closure I could bring to families and the idea of being able to take an offender off of the streets and put them behind bars was something I realized I wanted to do for the rest of my life. This newfound love for forensic science was only intensified by the presence of true crime television shows such as *Criminal Minds, CSI,* and *NCIS,* as well as true crime novels (both fiction and nonfiction). The more crime that was revealed and portrayed, the more I wanted to time travel so I could be working in a lab at that exact moment.

I didn't want to do forensic science for just any lab. I quickly determined that I wanted to work for the Federal Bureau of Investigation. The FBI has a rigorous training process, which requires not only a bachelor's degree, but strongly suggests having a master's, as well as having a mandatory two years at the FBI's new agent training academy in Quantico, Virginia. The academy requires both physical and educational excellence in order to be considered for the FBI upon completion of the term.

Even after the honor of becoming an official FBI agent, there is a lot one must do to keep the position and prove that one deserves it. Agents do not really get a say in where they are sent; however they do get to request a few field offices where they would prefer to be stationed. There are field offices in almost every major city, which makes sense because of crime rates in metropolitan areas.

Most people would be put off by how many years of schooling is necessary for this specific career path, but I have always enjoyed school and learning. I've always felt it is extremely important to never stop feeding my intelligence through education, even if that means changing my interests or what I was studying. I have even debated in my mind how to continue to earn degrees after entering my field of work so I can always be climbing the ladder of education.

Because of this intense love for learning, I realized quickly that I also was deeply interested in the mind and human behavior. This fascination led me to the choice of a double major in college in both biology and criminal psychology. The psychology degree opened my eyes to the possibility of criminal profiling, which I now realize is something I would very much like to do. Yes, profiling does not require laboratory sciences like forensic science does, but it is still a science—just a behavioral one. Profiling is also a discipline that can be studied at the FBI Academy, and if I choose that path, I will continue to pursue my dream of working for the FBI, although being unsure of the exact position.

I now have the opportunity to choose between two career paths: criminal profiling or forensic science. If given the chance, I would gladly jump at the possibility of doing both. Because I have chosen to do both of these majors, I have a broader spectrum of professions into which I can go. Perhaps when I enter graduate school for my master's degree, then I will decide that I would prefer to do neuropsychology or some other form of science, but that is the beauty of having both. It seems like a lot, and honestly, sometimes I get overwhelmed, but then I look at the bigger picture I am working on completing and I realize it is all going to be worth it.

I don't think there is any other path of life I would like to continue, even though I know this path is going to require a lot of work. There will always be ups and downs in life, but I have never been as excited for something in my future than I am for the feeling of satisfaction I will get from helping close criminal cases.

Angel Garrett is a junior from Eudora, Kansas. She is a member of the Ottawa University cheerleading team, president of the Biology Club, and a member of Sigma Alpha Alpha. Angel has a double major in biology and applied criminal psychology and plans to graduate in the spring of 2022. After graduation, Angel intends to apply to graduate school before attending the FBI Academy.

BRYNDEN GROW

I didn't understand what a liberal arts education was until I attended Ottawa. After attending for almost three years now, I am starting to understand what exactly it is. A liberal arts education is one that better prepares the student for life. From our motto, "Prepare for a life of significance," I believe Ottawa is doing just that. While still allowing me to focus on my degree, I am gaining more knowledge outside of it as well through my liberal arts studies. Attending here has really broadened my perspective of how I see the world.

Being here has put in many critical thinking classes that have helped me learn how to solve issues more quickly and come up with solutions to complex problems. It's not about the knowledge I've gained here, but the relationships and connections I've made here which are going to be ones that will be with me for the rest of my life.

Ottawa has also emphasized the importance of looking at my future as well. With having classes that teach me how to make connections, have a wonderful resume, and make sure I get the job I want, my future look bright for life after college. I'm excited about my future. After OU, I want to go to another school to earn my degree in atmospheric science while having a job in the communications field. My dream is to be a chief meteorologist at a television station somewhere in the Midwest. I love the tornadoes, blizzards, and summer droughts a little too much to move anywhere else.

I want to thank Justin Clarke who has been a great overseer of our Top Scholars group. I also want to thank my academic advisor and teacher, Dr. Ryan Louis. He has not only taught me about life, but he's becoming a friend I'll always be able to go back to for help in the future. That being said, I'm going to expand on all of this throughout my submission to this year's edition. I'm grateful for this opportunity to write this and hope you enjoy my entry as well.

In my opinion, a liberal arts education has multiple purposes. One purpose is gaining a broader scope of knowledge. Attending OU as compared to a non-liberal arts college, my general knowledge of a broad range of subjects will be better. Of course, every school wants its students to succeed after their time is over at the university. However, here in Ottawa something feels different. The teachers really believe in the liberal arts. I've not just learned the geography of the world or the history of Kansas, but I have heard its stories from professors like Dr.

Folke. He's studied in places like Germany and was at the Berlin Wall when it was taken down. He even has a piece of it in his basement. Students just don't get teachers like that everywhere. That's a good example of the great faculty we have here.

We can also consider my professor, Dr. Ryan Louis, as another example. He's told me stories about his life growing up, how he worked for MTV, living in New York and then moving to Kansas where he's been for a long time now. He likes to bring real-life problems into class so we can apply our studies to them. And it doesn't have to be our teachers either, it can be people we've met along the way. Jon Niccum taught a media writing class here for a semester and I was fortunate enough to be part of it. Jon is a writer for the *Kansas City Star* and has interviewed almost everyone you can think of in the entertainment industry. One big name that pops out to me is Stan Lee, the founder of the Marvel empire. As I said, it's not just the classes we take that give us more knowledge. It's the teachers' lives, the speakers who come through town, or a volunteer day sponsored by the university.

Our classes are our main means by which we learn things. Even though others find it annoying they have to take a class that has nothing to do with their major, I find it beneficial because I'm learning something new. Who knows, I may somehow be able to relate that to my field of studies. One class I thought we very beneficial to me was a basic economics class. We followed along with Dave Ramsey's *College Guide to Economics* and I learned more about money in that class than I ever did in high school.

Another class in which I learned a lot was a course called "The Tales and Tombs of Scotland." In the course, which was taught by Andy Hazucha and Dr. Fish-Greenlee, we read books about the Orkney Islands in the northern isle of Scotland. In these stories, we learned about the Vikings who lived there over time, how a girl from Orkney traveled to the mainland, and about all of the different tombs and history that is part of Orkney's past. We were also supposed to travel to the Orkney Islands but that was around the time when COVID hit and ruined our plans for 2020 and 2021. I hope they consider the trip in the spring of 2022. That class helped me form a connection with a brewery in Orkney and a local brewery here in Ottawa. It was neat to compare the two and see how the process at both places vary one from another.

I've talked about some classes but I haven't yet mentioned my major classes. I attribute that to the fact that we learn more than just information in our major when attending a liberal arts college. Let's talk about my major for a quick second. I'm a communications major with a focus in speech. If you remember, earlier I wrote I wanted to go to another school after Ottawa and get my degree in atmospheric science. So how do the two meet in the middle?

Basically, graduating with my major from Ottawa, I will be able to report and broadcast weather to the world. With my degree in atmospheric science, I can take that to another level and work with bigger companies that deal with the weather. The dream company for me would probably be Accuweather because it reports on so much stuff, not just around the U.S., but also around the world. I'm always open to learn more about the world and that is a place that would allow me to do so. This is in part why I'm excited about my future after my time here at Ottawa is done.

Before I talk about my future, I want to mention another reason why a liberal arts education is important to me. Critical thinking has become an important part of my college career and that comes with being a Top Scholar and one of Dr. Louis' students. As a Top Scholar, we're supposed to be the best of the best. We're all the kids who think outside the box in a way. This submission in itself is a critical thinking project in its own right. As a critical thinker, I may be able to approach problems at a different level than others. When a few critical thinkers are in a room, a lot can get done. Everyone may take a different approach to the problem but when they collaborate, they will be able to solve that problem. I'm grateful I get to be taught a way of critical thinking that pertains to myself and not others. This is a tool in my bag that hopefully will continue to be sharpened throughout my life.

The future is scary, but if I'm not scared or nervous when thinking about the future, then something may be wrong. Of course, it's super exciting, but I don't know what can happen tomorrow as we learned during the pandemic. My future is still uncertain in some aspects. I don't know what school I would like to attend after Ottawa. I don't know what job I'm going to have. I don't know how I'm going to take care of myself. That's something I choose not to worry about right now. I'm in the present, so why I am worried about the future? I need to focus on the now so I can better ensure I won't worry as much.

Where did the idea of working for a weather company come from? I have always been fascinated with severe weather. My dad took me storm chasing when I was a baby and storms always had a way of making me happy back then. My favorite movie is the 1996 blockbuster film *Twister*, which starred the late great Bill Paxton. I grew to appreciate the beauty and power of some storms through that movie. I'm interested in the weather, but I have realized not a lot of people know much about it. They may know how a thunderstorm works or how rain drops from a cloud, but not very many people can explain how the air currents in a mesocyclone produce a tornado. That's where I want to come in and teach people about this stuff.

I've already done a little bit of that in my speech classes with Dr. Louis. I gave an informative speech about tornadoes and the intricacies occurring inside a storm that produce them. I also went over how the damage is calculated and from that, a rating is given to the tornado. I'm now writing a persuasive speech to try and influence my colleagues to become a SKYWARN Storm Spotter for the National Weather Service (NWS). I was excited to participate in a webinar class put on by the National Weather Service recently on how to become a storm spotter. I already have Dr. Louis joining me to do so. I must have intrigued him so much with my first speech that he wants to learn more about the weather—and that is my goal!

It would be fun to chase and report on storms like one of my idols Reed Timmer still does. He's revolutionized the storm chasing game by helping create new technology to better reveal what happens in storms. With this new technology, we can better predict when more severe weather can happen, which leads to better protection from Mother Nature to the population. In my ending to that speech about tornadoes, I said something along the lines of, "If I can help people stay safer from storms, then I'm going to do it to the best of my ability." I truly mean that. I want to help create change in some way in this world. I think doing it this way is in my best interest.

As I close, a liberal arts education means a few things to me. First, it allows me to gain a broader perspective and have a greater knowledge of the world. We gain information not just from class, but from the people around us, such as our colleagues and professors. Another purpose for a liberal arts education is to teach us critical thinking and how to use it. Being taught how to think critically can be a huge benefit and I see it enriching my future.

I'm excited about my future in the weather industry and dream about changing the world. I've thought about different career paths, but I think this one is truly meant for me. Ottawa has helped and continues to help me better myself and lead to a life of significance. I love going to school here; it has become my home away from home. I will always know I am welcome back to Ottawa when I leave. This school has captured my heart and I cannot wait to see what the future holds. Go Braves!

Brynden Grow is a junior at Ottawa University. He is a part of the men's bowling team and is a Presidential Top Scholar. Brynden is majoring in communications with a focus in speech. After graduation, he plans to enter a master's program at a yet-to-be-determined school.

DOMINIC WIMBUSH

To describe the purpose of an education within the field of liberal arts, I must first define what a liberal arts education is, and what it provides for individuals who choose to include it in their personal educational profile. A liberal arts education is that which delves into the social structures of the humanities, which is the way that people interact and create valuable impact and content in the world around them. People who seek this education are those who want to make a significant impact on the world around them, whether it be in business, technology, socialization and administration, or simply education as a field in itself. These are the people who are attracted to a college campus that provides liberal arts degrees. It is my job to offer my opinion as to the true purpose of modern liberal arts education, which I can simply say aligns with the definition.

Most people I know have multiple options as they apply to and then enroll college, and when they end up choosing a smaller, local college, they have done so for the education it provides in the terms of value. The quality of education matters to these individuals, and these same students tend to be the ones who are referred to in the above definition. They are students who want to create a world through their own vision that will benefit mankind and humanity, furthering their existence and the quality of life they enjoy. Ottawa University's motto is "preparing you for a life of significance." Thus the University attracts and then equips those individuals who want to align with that common goal and go on to do the same after graduation.

This is one reason why I made my decision to come to Ottawa to continue my education after high school. I discovered I was an individual with many passions, and I could not end up pursuing them all. After doing some searching within, I found the one thing that has always kept me interested throughout my life is dedication to the people around me who sought help. I am currently turning this passion into a degree at Ottawa through their communications department from which I am expecting to graduate in 2022.

I chose communications because it runs into and intersects every aspect of life. Everywhere we go, all the life we see relies on communication for survival. Without it, we would be lost, without the means of escaping our own ignorance. I chose to learn how to effectively communicate to anyone, anywhere in order to be able to bridge the obstacles between people that can be so easily overcome. After taking just a few courses, I learned communication isn't something that comes naturally to a lot of people. It has to be learned and refined over time, in different settings and with different audiences. I have also learned that communication isn't just verbal. Body language can sometimes speak louder than words, as well as facial expressions, tone and intonation, and voice inflection. All these play a vital role in having a complete and well-rounded knowledge of understanding for people in general.

Liberal arts education sets a foundation for our minds to grow and develop in many ways over time. This development allows us to learn and be better equipped with the knowledge to succeed over time. To establish a foundation of lifelong learning is what I have to need for my personal success journey. And being given the opportunity to better establish myself with a foundation of knowledge, then I need to make myself more rounded as an individual. That is what I have always needed to pursue my goals and make myself the man I want to be five to ten years from now. Then looking back, I want to have the knowledge of everything I'm doing for within my life. This sort of education helps one become more well-rounded so that opportunities are more available to us. Not only do we as liberal arts students go into more depth in a specific major subject, we also are exposed to a wide range of subjects to expand our knowledge of many areas of learning.

Some people may not like this approach, and it definitely isn't for everyone. For someone like me, we can agree that this is required to become a true professional in whatever field we may pursue as a career for the rest of our lives. When I think about high-achieving individuals, I think of those who have a grasp on how to get the most out of life as a whole—people that can really excel in whatever circumstances that they are given simply because they are prepared for it. This is the type of individual I seek to be, so this is why I applied to OU in the first place.

People had told me that college is not only about the education but also about how conducive the environment is in which we insert ourselves for growth and development as we find out the kind of people we truly are and who we want to be for the rest of our lives. We learn morality, decision making, professionalism, and critical thinking and problem solving withing the respective college campuses we choose. These are things that are truly priceless. Being able to make sensible decisions within our chosen profession is just the foundation for what is expected of us. We should push ourselves to make innovative and productive decisions to better ourselves and the business for which we work. I must learn to set standards for myself that will enable me not only to be competitive within my field, but also to be one of the best within my respective field.

If I do not strive for improvement and excellence every day, how do I expect to continue growing and improving as a person? It brings a sense of accomplishment and pride that I can't lose when I am seeking to do things right. When I try to do the bare minimum to get by, I make it known that I don't want to be where I am or do what I am doing. I should find a different career if that is the problem, something I can devote myself to, something I can be passionate about. If I allow myself to sink to mediocrity, I will never rise in the ranks of the professional world. It is simply too competitive these days.

Take the up-and-coming Esports Industry for example. This industry is quite competitive right now because there are a lot of people interested in it, and simply not enough spots for all of them. The skillsets someone has to have to make it into the industry have to be refined and elite. Any chance the players get could be their first—and last. The industry could even be known as "volatile" for this reason in general. People like me have an Esports dream and want to make it to professional play/or staff through the industry one day. To make it there, I would have to have a lot of experience, a great track record, and insane grit. Obtaining those things aren't easy, but educating myself is a great starting point to get me where I want to be.

That brings me back to the importance of a liberal arts education. Having these principles taught to you is incredibly important and useful when going into competitive industries such as the one I mentioned. They can really help someone out when they are trying to separate themselves from the rest of the pack.

What I'm most excited about in my future is to start being an adult. Some people wouldn't find this fun but being able to set out and set myself up in life is what defines classic American freedom. Being able to blaze my own path and experience life in general are things incredibly exciting to me. I haven't been passionate about the jobs I have had so far. Passion will be the fuel to drive my ambition. I am looking forward to life, and I am one who will make it what I will it to be.

My overall goal is to collect as much experience as possible within the Esports field throughout the rest of my educational career. I want to enter the Esports scene with a great background and some awesome connections within the industry to set me up for success when looking for a career at the collegiate level. Right now, I have done quite well building up my resume for what I want to do within the industry. I am one of the founding members for the Braves Esports Team on campus, as well as having two collegiate Overwatch competitive seasons of experience.

I now am the student head coach of our new League of Legends program, and handled recruiting and administrative duties. Speaking of administration, I am an administrator for our central hub of communication for the team through our Discord Server, as well as a roster administrator for an amateur league called Zero Gravity Gaming. I have gained experience working as a shoutcaster, production lead, and analyst. I'm looking forward to working with more and more wonderful people in the near future when it comes to Esports.

The real reason I am passionate about the Esports industry is because I believe it can be so much more than it is today. I want to keep improving myself by collecting more and more knowledge within the industry so I can set myself up for success when I reach that point in my life. I want to be able to influence younger audiences of future generations and show them how wonderful Esports can be as a whole. Being able to mold myself into a lifelong learner that will set me apart from the standard of mediocrity is very important to the success of my career path. The real goal is to be an influencer, to make an example of myself to show what people can do through hard work and perseverance as they dedicate themselves to the craft that they chose.

I had one professor tell me during a seminar for leadership that there are many people who waste their time trying to be good at everything, when true professionals are only good at one specific thing. If I can only truly master one thing, why not master myself? He who masters himself will never be mastered by anyone else. This is something I picked up from reading self-help books to make sense of things in life. Reading has been something that has dramatically changed my mindset for the better, and I believe reading for 15 minutes a day can helps people manage the mental luggage they carry throughout the day.

I hope someday I will have enough knowledge concerning success principles that I will be able to write and then publish a book of my own. Maybe I will be able to pass on the teachings others have given me to help others out there who need them the same way I needed them at the time. I'm incredibly grateful for the opportunity to continue my education here and to further myself as a person. Go Braves!

Dominic Wimbush is a junior from Ottawa, Kansas and is one of the founding members of Ottawa University's esports team, Braves Esports. He is majoring in communications with a focus on strategic communication. Following graduation, Dominic plans on joining the collegiate scene to coach League of Legends.

SECTION FOUR

  Graduating scholars are given a choice. They can either answer "How has Ottawa prepared you for a life of significance?" or submit a piece of coursework of which they are most proud. In either case, the results are interesting and illuminating.

  These pieces are all well worth the time it takes to read them for they highlight the work our Scholars are capable of doing as they leave our institution, ready to take their skills and knowledge wherever the wind of destiny takes them. These students have left their mark on Ottawa, and we are excited they are taking a piece of Ottawa with them as they intellectually cross-pollinate their surroundings as they move toward the bright futures which lay ahead of them.

JOE CORBIN

HOW HAS OTTAWA UNIVERSITY PREPARED YOU FOR A LIFE OF SIGNIFICANCE?

"I do not feel obliged to believe that the same God who has endowed us with sense, reason, and intellect has intended us to forgo their use."— Galileo Galilei, Letter to the Grand Duchess Christina

As a senior student who is ready to graduate from Ottawa University in the spring of 2021, I have found it is difficult to feel prepared for the uncertainty of the future. I do not know the trials, pains, failures, and successes that await me as I take the next steps in my journey to adulthood and—more importantly—to a life of significance. Then again, I think I sometimes misunderstand what it means to be prepared.

I often mistake the definition of preparedness to being certain of success, or at least success as defined by my surrounding culture. This is probably due to the educational example that being prepared for a test often means the test-taker will pass the test with flying colors. This analogy is then mistakenly carried over to other aspects of life. It is easy to believe that if we work hard enough, all our tests will be passed with ease and all our dreams fulfilled. It is easy to be convinced that our merit will entitle us to, and even guarantee, financial prosperity, a good education, a successful career, happy and fulfilled families, and spiritual growth.

People often look to examples of celebrities, business tycoons, professional athletes, and others who have become culturally significant because they have reached the height of performance in their field due to their hard work and preparation. But what does it *really* mean to be prepared? On the other side of the spectrum, an equally dangerous belief can take root; the idea that mere existence entitles us to success and significance. Both concepts differ in their level of preparedness, yet both share greed as their root.

There need only be one occurrence to disprove this proposition that preparedness automatically leads to success. The life event I have in mind is clear: tragedy. How can one be prepared for an unexpected tragedy? The death of a loved one, the diagnosis of a rare form of cancer, the loss of a stable job, or a theft that leaves you with nothing—these are some of the tragedies of life that challenge the notion that being prepared and working hard is a one-way ticket to whatever your heart desires.

Since life does not always work out that the way we hope or want, how can one be prepared for whatever life brings? I contend that the essence of being prepared is deeper than what we initially think and resembles how the meanings of success and significance are much deeper and elusive than what the surrounding culture suggests. Being prepared is an internal and external state of being such that a task is executed in accordance with the knowledge and wisdom required to complete or endure the task. Furthermore, the reaction to an anticipated action, event, or stimulus is peace of mind regardless of one's performance. Let's consider some examples to understand what I mean by this definition of preparedness.

In the example of the test, my tendency is to say that to be prepared means I passed my test. However, being prepared for a test means that the test-takers have done what they can to ready themselves for the test by reviewing the content of the test *and* being at peace with the fact that passing is desired but failing is possible. Furthermore, this comes with the understanding that if the test is failed, it does not mean that the test-taker has failed at life itself. Given this definition and example of preparedness, how can one be prepared for a test, or for the ups and downs of life?

There are two steps to follow when it comes to being prepared. The first is to gain knowledge, experience, and wisdom when not being tested. For example, in the case of a test, one must gather the content that will be on the test and store it to memory as knowledge. Then the knowledge must be applied in the form of repetitive practice with different types of questions.

To illustrate this, consider the example of learning simple mathematical operations such as exponents, addition, subtraction, multiplication, and division. To gain knowledge means to put to memory what each operation does. To gain experience is to work with different examples of mathematical operations and to practice them repeatedly. Wisdom comes when one learns to discern that there are oftentimes multiple ways to arrive at the same solution in arithmetic.

The second step of preparation is to make certain that your mind and heart have worked together to be at peace, regardless of the result. I appeal to both the mind, the logical center of the human being, and the heart, the metaphorical emotional center of the human being, because they must work in tandem. Without the heart, the mind would not know how to respond to external stimuli, especially anything that appears illogical. Without the mind, the heart would not be able to quell emotions that quickly get out of control.

Now, as a Christian, it is imperative to include the Holy Spirit in the second step. God's Spirit dwells in those who trust in Jesus Christ as both Savior and Lord of their lives. When the heart and the mind are at odds or have been deceived, it is important to have God's Spirit speak what is true into the heart and mind in exchange for what is false. Anyone who fails to consider the spiritual aspect of life suffers from an incomplete second step of preparation.

When life takes a turn for the worse and all is on the brink of utter gloom, where do we turn? When our emotions run amuck and our minds become deceived, who will tell us what is true in exchange for the lies that we believe? Do not misunderstand what I mean, for there are plenty of people who reject God who are incredibly successful in this world, but I believe that life apart from the one, true God is ultimately devoid of purpose and meaning and will end in misery.

Unfortunately, definitions do not answer the uncertainty about the future I still feel. Luckily, it just so happens that I have spent the last two decades—and especially the last four years—acquiring knowledge, gaining experiences, and developing wisdom. I call it *getting an education*. Life preparation, in my opinion, is what getting an education is all about.

Furthermore, getting an education does not look the same for any one person. For me, education comes on many levels—from the public school system, to various summer jobs, to my undergraduate education at Ottawa University. I have experienced enough educational and professional institutions to understand that there is more to life than I could ever fathom. However, the last four years at Ottawa University are by far the highlight of my overall education. By the standard of preparedness outlined in this essay, I believe Ottawa University has prepared me for a life of significance to the best of its ability.

My first extended experience at Ottawa University was a Top Scholars competition in November of 2016. After a full day of writing, oral responses, and meetings with top Ottawa University officials, I knew that Ottawa University was going to be a place where I would be challenged to grow in virtually every aspect of life. A few weeks later, I was informed I had received the Presidential Scholarship from the Top Scholars competition. I was honored and nervous for I knew that "when someone has been given much, much will be required in return" (Luke 12:48, NLT). I knew that as soon as I stepped on campus, I would be expected to serve as a faithful servant leader both by the University and by God. During the summer of 2017, I intentionally spent time preparing my heart, mind, and soul for the challenges and joys ahead.

My freshman year at Ottawa University was a whirlwind. It included a fully-loaded academic schedule—19 credit hours in the fall and 18 credit hours in the spring—to a plethora of extra-curricular involvement. I decided that year to get involved in ways I had never done before. Besides running on the track and cross-country teams, I helped found the OU Engineering Club, served on the FCA leadership team, and volunteered to help with Braving Discipleship—among other things. Even with all that, by the end of the year, I was hungry for more.

After feeling the call to dive deeper, I applied to become a resident assistant and an orientation leader. Both interviews were nerve-racking, more challenging than any interview I had ever experienced. However, I soon discovered that I had been selected to fill both positions. After another summer of preparation, I dove into an intense, two-week process of training in early August of 2018 for both positions. I was forced to learn quickly and think carefully about how I would resolve disputes and take care of the duties of both positions. By God's grace, I survived my initial term as an orientation leader and made some great connections with my group members that remain to this day.

Sophomore year challenged me more than I had ever been challenged. Between an exceedingly difficult load of mathematics and science courses and serving in more roles on campus than ever, I was genuinely concerned about how I would be able to take care of everything. Fortunately, I was surrounded by amazing family, friends, and staff who helped me and showed me grace in many ways. I was able to make it through my sophomore year despite the challenges I faced, so I took plenty of time to rest during the summer of 2019 before I re- entered the busy world I found myself in.

The start of my junior year in the fall of 2019 began on a low note with the loss of several faculty and staff at Ottawa who left to pursue other opportunities. Fortunately, that did not stop me from making the most of my second year as a resident assistant and orientation leader. Yet, there was one event that broke me. I had a resident, also named Joseph, who transferred to Ottawa for the school year. Like me, Joseph was a STEM student hoping to become a mathematics teacher. He was intelligent but did not have many friends that I could see. So, I made it my mission to talk with him and check up on him regularly.

One night, I was working at the Resident Assistant desk in Bennett Hall when I saw Joseph on his way out. I asked him how he was doing and what he was up to. He told me, with a smile on his face, that he was on his way to go hang out with a friend who lived close by. I smiled and wished him a good rest of his evening. The next day, I woke up and checked my email. I found an urgent message sent out by the OU Residence Life office asking that all resident assistants come to the Residence Life office immediately.

I got up out of bed, threw on some shorts and a t-shirt, and walked over to the office. As I was walking over, I saw a fellow Bennett Hall Resident Assistant walking back to his room. I asked him what happened, and he shook his head. I knew at that moment that I had to prepare myself for what I was about to hear. When I reached the office, I was informed that Joseph had died the night before.

The next few weeks were dreadful. I was not close to Joseph but it felt like I had lost someone I knew well. I carried this burden with me for the rest of the year. Even during the good times, like when I was serving as a coordinator for Braving Discipleship or serving as a Bennett Hall Representative in the OU Student Senate, that unfortunate event hung over me like a cloud. Regardless, I had to push forward, dependent upon the grace of God to carry me through the rest of the year.

One thing that helped lift me up were the opportunities before me. I was supposed to visit Israel with some of my best friends. I was supposed to go to Hawaii to see my older sister get married. I was supposed to return to school after spring break. These things were supposed to go as planned. Then, the COVID-19 pandemic hit the world hard. I was not fully prepared for so many negative things to happen within a matter of a half of a year, but what preparation I had done paid off—and is paying off still.

I had prepared my heart, mind, and soul for situations where life seemed gloomy and unfair by remembering the truth of God's goodness and sovereignty. Fortunately, I still had my core group of loving and supportive family and friends around me who helped me through the difficult moments. This preparation was accomplished while I was at Ottawa University, amid many challenges in almost every aspect of my life.

As stated before, I believe that to be prepared is an internal and external state of being such that a task is executed in accordance with the knowledge and wisdom required to complete or endure the task and that the reaction to an anticipated action, event, or stimulus is peace of mind regardless of performance. That may sound like an overly complicated definition, but I was not satisfied with other definitions I had seen suggesting that preparation means "being ready for something." While not necessarily an incorrect definition, it simply does not dive deep enough in my opinion.

As for the uncertainties that the future may hold, bring them on. I trust that God has prepared me and is still preparing me for what will come. And I believe God used Ottawa University, its students, faculty, and staff, to prepare me for life. This life may or may not appear to be significant to the wider culture, but it will be a life that will be used significantly for God's glory among all nations.

Thank you Mom, Dad, Lauren, and Emily. Your unending love and support helped me not only survive but also thrive throughout my experience at Ottawa University. Thank you Garrett, Morgan, Joseph, Will, Bobby, Caleb, Daniel, and so many other amazing friends who have helped bring joy to my life. Thank you, Dr. Sonja Flesberg, for your care, honesty, and willingness to expand the minds of your students with examples that made learning fun. Thank you, Professor Grigsby, for constantly challenging me to think about the world and its many problems differently. Thank you Dr. Justin Clarke, for your leadership among the Top Scholars group and for being an outstanding professor who helps teach students how to think logically and philosophically. Thank you OU ResLife for the amazing two years as a Resident Assistant.

Thank you to Ottawa University's Hetrick Bistro and the maintenance and custodial staff for always putting a smile on my face. Finally, I thank God for the opportunity to attend Ottawa University. I pray that He will bless the University, not for its sake, but for the sake of the future OU Braves who will have a college experience like none other. May they experience His goodness as I have.

Joe Corbin is a graduating senior from Edgerton, Kansas. He is president of the Ottawa University Sigma Alpha Alpha Honor Society, competes for the Ottawa University men's track and cross country teams, and is a member of the servant leadership teams for both Chi Alpha Campus Ministries and Fellowship of Christian Athletes at Ottawa University. Joe is majoring in engineering and graduated in May of 2021. After graduation, Joe hopes to become a project engineer for a local engineering firm and to dedicate his life to the service of God and humanity.

MEGHAN CUBBISON

ART THERAPY: A BETTERMENT TO MENTAL HEALTH BEHIND BARS

Table of Contents

Introduction
    Literature Review

Section I: Inmates and Mental Health
    Prison Systems in America
    Inmates and Mental Health Disorders

Section II: Art Therapy
    Types of Art Therapy
    Benefits of Art Therapy in Prison

Section III: Case Studies
    California Institution for Women
    New Jersey Correctional Institution for Women
    David Gussak's FSU Study
    California Arts-In-Corrections Program
    Rikers Island Department of Corrections

Summary

Works Cited References

LITERATURE REVIEW

The issue of mental health is a prevalent matter in the American prison system, so much so that it's reported in jails in America, one in five inmates suffer from diagnosed mental illness—as do 15% of all inmates in American prisons. This number shows there is 10 times more mentally ill inmates than there are patients in America's remaining psychiatric hospitals (Carroll, 2106). This poses as an issue for the inmate as shown in research stating that prisoners in one state prison remained incarcerated longer than those who are not suffering from a mental illness.

Another issue with mental health in jails and prisons in this country is the cost of living through community resources so that prisons can provide some form of medication to these inmates. Because of this, inmates with mental health issues cost more to imprison than those who do not suffer from these same challenges (Carroll, 2016). With such a serious issue as this, one would hope there is is a relative, effective solution to the problem.

Art therapy is the use of artforms and media in a way that is therapeutic and can relate to one's underlying diagnosis of mental health disorders. Art therapy can be used to work through traumas such as PTSD and abuse as well as a way to release dopamine into the brain to counteract illnesses such as depression and anxiety. As I begin, let's take a look at one of the most common mental illnesses in America: depression.

The biological factors of depression include a lack of a chemical called serotonin to the brain. This chemical is sent in what is called a neurotransmitter to other neurotransmitters as well as the brain (Nemade, 1995). Art therapy is one way to cope with and treat depression. In art therapy, it is important to consider that there is no particular artform that works better than another, but rather the importance lies in the comfortability in the artist. Art therapy presented or facilitated by a licensed therapist can be beneficial since a licensed therapist can tailor the therapy to meet a patient's specific needs. The goals of art therapy include but are not limited to managing behaviors, processing feelings, reducing stress and anxiety, and heightening self-esteem (www.rotor.org, 2020).

Well-known inmate and serial killer John Wayne Gacy was on death row in an Indiana prison in 1982. He was convicted of torturing, killing, and raping more than 33 young men and male children. During his incarceration, he created a series of paintings and art on nearly 2,000 canvases until he was executed by lethal injection in 1994. The paintings consisted of a wide variety of depictions including self-portraits of his alter persona, "Pogo the Clown," to Disney characters such as the dwarves in the movie *Snow White*—and even human anatomy.

Just before his death sentence, nearly three dozen of Gacy's pieces were sold by the Tatou Art Gallery in Beverly Hills, CA, the most expensive one selling for $20,000. One of Gacy's most famous pieces is one titled "Sex Skull," which is a depiction of a human skull composed of male and female genitals ("John Wayne Gacy's"). If a mentally unstable individual as Gacy can obtain psychological benefits from art while incarcerated, whether he was on death row or not, one can only imagine the betterment that art therapy could provide for inmates who are also mentally unstable yet are attempting to reintegrate into society.

So how does art therapy pertain to the mental health of those facing incarceration, or better yet, from where did the passion behind this topic emanate? While there may not be much research on the matter, art therapy in prison not only aids in the betterment of prisoner's behavior overall, but also can help by assisting the prisoners with life goals and skills that can be used outside of prison post-incarceration.

According to research in America, recidivism or re-offenses among federal inmates in America is up to 45%, meaning that nearly half of all inmates are repeat offenders of crime (Keller, 2016). Programming such as GED and life skills programming in prisons is shown to lower recidivism since inmates without a high school education are ten times more likely to reoffend than those who have graduated with a high school diploma.

Does age play a factor into recidivism? Those released before age 21 have a 68 percent likelihood of reoffending (Keller, 2016). With as many inmates as there are who consistently reoffend after release, could there be programing that would give inmates a chance to positively reconnect with their community and provide them with skills and resources to utilize outside of prison? There is and art therapy is one of them.

This is where art therapy plays a role in the prison system by reducing mental illness, addressing behavioral issues and more for those behind bars—not to mention reducing recidivism. Not only has art therapy been proven to therapeutically aid mental health disorders in prison such as depression, anxiety and PTSD, but it also has been proven to lessen behavioral issues and write ups for behavioral incidents that stem from these mental health disorders. This shortens sentences as well as time spent in solitary isolation (Colorado, 2016). The Women's

Division of the Colorado State Penitentiary is one prison in particular that has used art therapy since 1965 as a way for inmates to express hardships in a healthy manner such as when incarceration creates forcible separation from their children.

SECTION I

As of research published in March of 2020, the American criminal justice system held nearly 2.3 million people in a combination of 1,833 state prisons, 110 federal prisons, 1,772 juvenile correctional facilities, 3,134 local jails, 218 immigration detention facilities, and 80 Indian Country jails and military prisons, civil commitment centers, state psychiatric hospitals, and prisons in the U.S. territories (Citation). As for why these people are incarcerated, one in five incarcerated inmates are locked up for a drug offense. On any given day, that is 450,000 nonviolent drug offenders who are incarcerated.

Other significantly represented offenses include those who committed violent crimes such as assault, robbery and murder, property crimes such as theft, and public order crimes including DUI's (Wagner, 2020). As we discuss the term "inmate" throughout this paper, it is important for the reader to understand that the word itself is not more closely associated with a specific socioeconomic, race, or diversified background, but rather, an inmate can be someone from a wide diversity of backgrounds (Brinkman, 2017).

There are many factors in the prison system that come into play for inmates who suffer from serious mental illnesses. One of these factors is that statistics show that inmates suffering from mental illness tend to have longer stays in inmate facilities.

> "In Florida's Orange County Jail, the average stay for all inmates is 26 days; for mentally ill inmates, it is 51 days. In New York's Riker's Island, the average stay for all inmates is 42 days; for mentally ill inmates, it is 215 days" (Carroll, 2016).

This may occur for many different reasons, the first being that most inmates with mental illnesses find it difficult to follow and abide by jail and prison rules. Some research shows that these inmates are twice as guilty of a rules' infraction than other inmates, while other research shows that in Washington State prisons, even though 19% of inmates suffer from a mental illness, they are responsible for nearly 41% of total infractions.

If the inmates are awaiting trial, it may take extra time for them to be incarcerated if they require an evaluation or restoration of competency to be able to stand trial. In most of these instances, inmates spend more time behind bars waiting for their competency restoration than they would spend behind bars for their actual sentence (Carroll, 2016).

Not only do mentally ill inmates remain behind bars longer, but more often than not they cost more to house in prisons than inmates who don't suffer from serious mental illness. In a 2003 study of Texas prisons, "the average prisoner costs the state $22,000 a year, but prisoners with mental illness range from $30,000 to $50,000 a year." What causes these inflated costs of housing and living in prisons?

A large part of it has to do with psychiatric medications. Another reason would be the costs of settling or paying for lawsuits that arise from the mistreatment of these mentally ill inmates. Due to their behavior, many times inmates suffering from severe mental illness can often wind up in isolation due to behavioral issues and misconduct. In a 2010 audit of state prisons, research found that between 55% to 76% of inmates in solitary confinement were in fact mentally ill.

Lastly, inmates suffering from forms of mental illness are more likely to be representative of the number of inmates who commit suicide every year. Suicide in prison is a major issue and is the leading cause of death for inmates to this day. Research shows that nearly half of all inmate suicides are committed by the 15%-20% of the prison population reported to have some sort of mental illness (Carroll, 2016).

Without a doubt, we can see that mental illness is a prevalent issue for men, women, and juveniles behind bars. Just as it would be in the outside world, serious mental illnesses such as depression can be dangerous if allowed to continue without treatment. This is one reason why many prisons have therapy and workforce programming within their walls. The primary focus of this paper is to highlight one of these forms of therapy used in many different prison systems, namely art therapy. In the next section of this paper, we will discuss what in fact art therapy is as well as its benefits in the lives of incarcerated inmates.

SECTION II

Therapy, though different for many people, can be a common treatment for people, inmates or not, who suffer from a wide variety of mental illnesses. Art therapy is, in its most simple context, "the application of visual arts, in a therapeutic context" (reading 3). These visual arts include a wide variety of creative expressions such as painting, drawing, ceramics, theater, photography, design, crafts, and architecture. Art therapy is not always administered by a licensed therapist, though there are benefits if it is.

The most important aspect of art therapy is the results one obtains that are beneficial to one's mental health as well as the comfort level one has with the chosen artistic component. For instance, if someone doesn't feel comfortable with their own artistic ability, then perhaps they should try journaling or fictional writing instead. One of the most important factors of art therapy if it is to help fight against mental illnesses like depression is its practice as a group activity. This helps establish and build healthy connections with people other than the inmate.

Research shows there are many benefits when it comes to inmates participating in art therapy. These can include aiding in issues of self-worth, confidence, and empowerment (Brewster, 2014). Not only are there emotional benefits to performing art therapy, but there is research suggesting physical and psychological benefits as well. This research shows a link between a development of the right brain through arts education and practice. This then leads to more focused attention, higher-order thinking skills, creativity, intellectual flexibility, the ability to work with others, self-discipline, and patience.

A major takeaway from art therapy for inmates is that it creates a fine-tuned sense of focus and discipline. A skilled mindset is required when an inmate pursues the precision that goes into the art, whether it be capturing an image for a photograph or a painting, finding the right words to fit a poem, or hitting the note or que for a performance. All those require a skillful mindset. There's also a benefit of satisfactory work with a finished product, be it a song, poem, or other art piece. Life skills such as a willingness to experiment and learning from mistakes, self-criticism, and self-reflection can also be obtained through the kind of work inmates put into their creative pursuits (Brewster, 2014).

Participation in art therapy can also lead to success in other areas of prison life, such as a more successful educational program. Those who have previously been alienated from the educational system may find reassurance through the nontraditional curriculum or teaching methods that art therapy has to offer. By allowing inmates to form positive relationships with their art instructors, inmates are also shown equal respect as artists rather than as persons with lessened authority. A 2007 study showed that inmates who participated in their facility's theater program were more likely to re-engage in GED and even college classes. Participation in prison art programs can also lead to a better overall solution to behavioral issues for inmates.

One benefit that many people may not realize from art therapy is that it can reconnect the inmates with their community in a positive way. This can be done by a number of ways. The first being that on occasion, inmates can sell their art for auction to members of their community. Where might the money go? Most of the time it goes to benefit local nonprofit organizations. Inmate art such as murals can also be used for community beautification. Another way inmates can connect with their community is through theater, performances of music, or even intimate prose and poetry readings (Brewster, 2014).

SECTION III

Little did we know that today there are strong art programs within many prison facilities in America. One we will be observing in this thesis is that of Project CULTURE, one of the first fully-funded programs designed by the American Correctional Association with the intention "to serve adult offenders in long-term state correctional facilities with quality activities; reduce tension levels and behavioral infractions in the institutions, and generate a greater community awareness of offenders and the correctional system through the participation of artists, guests and audiences" (Worall and Koines, 1978). Not only does Project CULTURE aid in the correctional requirements of incarceration, but also in many if not all judicial requirements in attempt to contribute to the "humanization of the institutional environment" (Worall and Koines, 1978).

CALIFORNIA INSTITUTION FOR WOMEN AT FONTERA (CIW)

In Los Angeles, California, Artists in Prison and Other Places, Inc. (AIPOP) has been bringing the experience of art to those in prison as well as those in hospitals since 1992. Project CULTURE contracted AIPOP in July of 1977 to provide a theater workshop as a program for the California Institution for Women at Fontera. The objective of this project was simple: to deinstitutionalize the women of the facility by allowing them the space to create and perform an original play to a select audience of the community.

There were also issues within the institution that created objectives for this project, such as creating a bond between the varied groups of women housed in the prison since there was widespread racial discord. There was a long list of benefits this program created including but not limited to:

1. one college credit obtained by each participant from LaVerne College;
2. a nationally televised feature of the workshop by Newsweek News Service;
3. a number of communal participants attended the sessions;
4. media coverage included articles in the *LA Times* and other local Southern California papers as well as a photographic essay produced by Judith Pacht and AIPOP which was exhibited in the GSA building in Washington D.C. for the National Exhibition of the American Correctional Association.

Not only was this theater program a success within the California Institution for Women at Fontera, but it's success also called for AIPOP to aid in the planning of a statewide arts program in Corrections with the State Department of Corrections in California.

So how did this program work itself out? Operationally, the writing and creating of the show was done in the education building of the CIW, while the dancing and the learning of acting techniques was done in a small auditorium on site. Classes were held at night, with writing sessions offered on Mondays, dance on Tuesdays, and performance on Thursdays. As always, there were problematic encounters for the workshop participants, including communication problems between CIW staff. This was resolved throughout the project, as well as two prison-wide lockdowns which hindered the allowance of practice at both the beginning and the end of the project. Not only did the success of the program bring the performance of an original piece by the incarcerated women, but also a deeper understanding by each of their own capabilities and skill sets.

Community members who were in the audience of the performance titled LINES were drawn from several mailing lists, including AIPOP and Mark Taper Forum Theater in Los Angeles along with more than 20 different colleges, universities, and community groups in Southern California. Most all these participants had never been inside of a prison before, and to heighten their experience and give them a glimpse of what it was like to live an incarcerated life, they had to undergo several general clearances including a full body and metal detector search.

There was positive feedback as a result to the CIW theater program among inmates, the facility itself, as well as the community surrounding CIW. As for the inmates, this programming allowed for "commitment, discipline, and creative self-expression" (Worall and Koines, 1978). The prison was also able to compile other methods of measurement such as test scores which also seemed to improve for inmate participants. The affirmation from community members also created an increased feeling of self-worth and accomplishment.

Not only did the facilities activity directors decide to continue with AIPOP's work, but they also desired to expand on what it had to offer, showing a fuller awareness of inmate needs. During the performance of LINES from April 11-16, more than 1,000 community members witnessed the work of the 28 inmates putting on the production. These community members came from the following organizations:

> UCLA, UC-Irvine, USC, Cal State-Long Beach, LaVerne College, Chapman College, Mount San Antonio College, Coastline Community College, San Diego State University, Cypress College, Friends Outside, Women's Building, Mark Taper Forum Theatre staff, Older Women's Liberation, and the Women's Center/ Orange Coast College (Worall and Koines, 1978).

NEW JERSEY CORRECTIONAL INSTITUTION FOR WOMEN

Project CULTURE was brought to the New Jersey Correctional Institution for Women in an effort to replace the dying art and music program within the facility. The pre-existing programs were defunded due to budget cuts in the 1970s. This facility is a minimum-security facility and houses approximately 240 inmates. During the beginning of Project CULTURE, they even took some low-risk male inmates in an attempt to battle the overcrowding of prisons occurring at that time.

At this particular institution, a number of leisurely activities were offered through Project CULTURE: creative writing, dance, music/chorus, music/movement/theater, along with art programs such as ceramics, weaving, sculpture, painting, printmaking, crafts, needlework and drawing—as well as a clown workshop (Worall and Koines, 1978).

The effectiveness of the programs was very high: "There are a few tests that can be administered to a creative writing class, or chorus, or dance that can measure the success rate. If the dance recital could be considered a 'test' then all the participants got an 'A.' If the poetry and prose that resulted from the creative writing workshops is a test, again an 'A.'" (Worall and Koines, 1978).

Not only did the participants excel on their own, but those in the music workshops even mustered the courage to sing in front of other inmates within the facility. As for the behavior of inmates within the workshops, there were no reports of infractions behaviorally or among multiple inmates during the duration of the workshops. Even those who did not participate in the workshops seemed to have better behaviors due to the influence of their peers who did participate.

There was also positivity spread through the murals the Art Programs painted on the walls of the facility as well as the affirmation given to inmates who performed in front of their peers. Not only that, but positive relations have also been created between inmates and their correctional officers. Many officers rearranged their schedules to be on duty during inmate performances, and the positive affirmation not only created respect for inmates from officers but also respect for officers from inmates as well.

Any issues that were encountered were said to have occurred at the beginning of the process, and that its success occurred most often as Project CULTURE remained an integral part of the facility at hand. Suggestions included night workshops so as not to interfere with job assignments or class times, as well as an orientation period for the art teachers to become acclimated to prison rules and expectations of inmates. It should also be noted that the benefits of this project were not only engrained in the minds of the inmates, but in those of the officers on staff as well. When being made aware of the positive outcomes of inmate involvement, the officer may be more apt to encourage such involvement to other inmates.

DAVID GUSSAK'S FSU STUDY ON REDUCING DEPRESSION IN PRISON

In 2007, David Gussak produced a literary journal article titled *The Effectiveness of Art Therapy in Reducing Depression in Prison Populations*. Gussak has been studying criminal counseling for years and has published works from as early as 1997. His reasoning behind art therapy is that inmates tend to suffer from other disorders such as illiteracy and lack of organicity, which create more significant barriers when attempting to communicate mental, emotional, and even psychological problems. This can make successful treatment for inmates an even more difficult goal to reach.

In this case study, the Formal Elements Art Therapy Scale (FEATS) was used to measure progress within inmates behaviors and tendencies in the production of their art. The study was conducted in a facility with medium to maximum security. The study also took place in a rural Florida facility. The mental health counselor of the facility chose 48 inmates to participate in the four-week period of services, including two group sessions per week. Participants ranged in age from 21 to 63 years of age.

For approximately 44% of the participants, this was their first sentence to a prison facility. The crimes committed by the participants that landed them in prison ranged from larceny to murder. All of the participants had an "Axis I diagnosis such as dysthymia or bipolar disorder, manic type" (Gussak, 2007, p. 447). All the participants had already taken part in counseling sessions in the day-treatment unit of the prison and the art therapy sessions counted as part of their preexisting treatments. Over half of the participants, approximately 51%, were also receiving psychotropic medications.

CALIFORNIA ARTS-IN-CORRECTIONS PROGRAM (AIC)

In this particular study, attitudinal and behavioral changes were measured. The prisons participating in this study included the California Rehabilitation Center (CRC) in Norco, San Quentin State Prison, the Correctional Training Facility (CTF) in Soledad, and New Folsom State Prison. Participation ranged from acting, to Shakespeare appreciation, to visual arts, to poetry and writing courses. The percentage of participation by prison was 32.8% of CRC inmates, 27.9% of Folsom inmates, 26.2% of Soledad inmates, and 13.1% of San Quentin inmates.

Two male inmate populations participated in the study by taking classes through the California Arts-In-Corrections (AIC) program. The AIC was formed in 1980 and existed until 2010 when it was eliminated due to budgeting issues. The AIC at one point was able to offer classes to each of the state prisons in music, writing, visual arts, theater, and other fine arts programs. The amount of time spent by these men in the AIC program was 1-33 years, with an average participation of 6.4 years. Less than 18% of the participants participated for less than a year, 26% participated for 2-4 years, and over 56% participated for more than five consecutive years. Nearly half of the men participated in music studies, three-quarters participated in writing and/or poetry classes, 20% took theater classes, and nearly half participated in some form of visual arts. It should be noted that the total percentage exceeds 100%, because several of the men participated in multiple art forms (Brewster 2014).

The men participated in AIC for many different reasons. Some wanted to better themselves and their behavior, some simply wanted to learn a new set of skills, while others wanted to be able to have something they could share with their families. Some were curious or had always enjoyed art. Most of the participants, whether they stayed in for five years or less than a year, said that their participation helped them "express themselves, relieve stress, feel happier, be creative, and to make better choices ...Art helps them to better understand themselves and to work with others (Brewster, 2014).

Over half of the inmates said that while pursuing art they were able to get along better with other inmates in the facility. Those with more than two years of participation proved to have better relationships with the prison staff and began to form a better understanding of their self-worth. Out of the men who remained in the program for more than five years, 65% got along better with other inmates, 61% liked themselves more, 61% had fewer disciplinary records, 52% got along with staff better, and 30% got along better with family members.

Study numbers were even taken from non-AIC participants and showed that 49% had never studied or practiced art in the past; 5% studied art prior to incarceration; 26% practiced art prior to incarceration; and 20% both studied and practiced art prior to incarceration. Of these inmates, 96% very much enjoyed the art classes and 95% definitely wanted to take another art class in the future.

The AIC participants then responded to a survey consisting of 33 questions which included the LEQ attitudinal scales. The pre-test had 28 questions and the post-test had 30 questions. Both descriptive and comparative statistics were used for this survey. The theater, visual arts, and poetry classes were observed by an investigator who was able to interview several of the participants. The whole goal of the study was to obtain information correlating the creative processes positively with skills of life effectiveness that could be measured by the attitudinal scales. This was found through the finding that "successful problem solving requires creative, flexible, and innovative thinking which depends on a well-developed and active right brain" (Brewster, 2014).

Self-confidence, achievement motivation, time management, and emotional control and social competence were all measured through the survey. For self-confidence, research showed that those who partook in art therapy had a better understanding of self-appreciation and worth. They also tended to believe more in the idea that their creative mind opened them up to a world full of creative possibilities as compared to those who did not partake in art therapy. Many of the men found and learned that hard work pays off through the projects they created, which allowed them to find motivation through their work.

Research also showed that practicing and studying art had a positive correlation to self-management and self-discipline, both of which are prerequisites to successful time management skills. Since prison is primarily focused on the inmates constraining their own time, those who were interviewed after participating in AIC's art programs found themselves more apt to manage their time behind bars better.

According to Brewster's article, social and emotional development are shown to be strongly linked. With social development being prevalent in the prison system, it is important that inmates have the ability to control their emotions as well. Art is the perfect method of emotional and creative expression. Social competency also accompanied the many skills gained from participating in art therapy. Those who participated in AIC programs said they felt more comfortable navigating social situations and felt as if communication with others improved as well. The self-expression did not just come from deciding what instrument to play, or what project to make and what materials to be used in a said project, but also in the fact that it allowed them to make these decisions, giving them their first chance to make actual decisions behind bars. For one individual, emotional control was found through the ability to reconnect with his sons. He shared:

> What the Arts-in-Corrections program did, I think, was give me and my boys something to talk about in the visiting room . . . a topic of conversation other than the idle or awkward chit-chat you so often hear among families during visitation. We'd draw pictures on napkins and talk about fine art and my guitars and music. Because I was enrolled in other art courses, it wasn't just the guitars we talked about. There was always something of interest that helped us to communicate and that made my boys proud of me… they could talk with their friends about how their dad made guitars and painted pictures . . . they showed their friends the guitars I made for them, and eventually they learned to play, and today one is a musician and the other helps me in my business. They tell me it helped to erase the stigma of having their father in prison (Brewster, 2014).

Statistically speaking, inmates who participated in AIC's programming were nearly 10% more likely to want to continue with regular education after their art courses were complete even though those who participated were also 20% more likely to have previously pursued education prior to the programming.

The findings of this research go to show that there is a positive correlation between art therapy and improvement of many inmate issues. Not only does it improve their mood as well as their sense of self-worth, motivation, and emotional expression, but it also allows for them to form more coherent relationships with their fellow inmates, their prison staff, and even their communities.

RIKERS ISLAND DEPARTMENT OF CORRECTIONS (DOC)

Art therapists Lesley Achitoff and Katie Hinson worked closely with some of Rikers Island's most troubled inmates in an effort to offer hope to those inmates through their practices. The inmates, or rather, patients as they are referred to by the therapists, met with Hinson every weekday in three to four different one-hour group sessions. When the group started, the patients were waiting for her in the dayroom. Hinson lets the patients pick out music to listen to while they worked, otherwise they wouldn't get to choose much of anything in the position they were in.

Art therapy was an optional elective for these inmates in Rikers "mental observation unit" (Thackara, 2016). The materials that Achitoff and Hinson relied on wee what artists consider "dry mediums: oil and chalk pastels, coloring pens and pencils, and materials for collage" (Thackara, 2016). Achitoff went on to explain why putting loose materials or paint on the table for inmates to use may have been detrimental to a patient with mental illness(es).

She explains how it can be dis-regulating to the patient, especially those coming from a traumatic background, as it can act as a trigger. "Wet materials are more emotionally charged . . . and their very nature as liquids makes them more prone to accidents. Patients will sometimes become more overwhelmed if they do something wrong" (Thackara, 2016). Paint is one of the more common materials to end up as a form of contraband, therefore, when it goes missing from the rest of the art supplies, patients may have to undergo a series of strip searches, which are an invasion of privacy.

What might make paint a contraband, you may ask? In an environment like prison where self-expression and creativity are limited to just therapy purposes only, an inmate may feel compelled to smuggle paints in order to color their hair or nails outside of therapy. Scissors, tape, and stickers are also in the category of banned supplies. For projects such as collages, inmates will receive pre-cutout magazine images to collage together. They are also encouraged to use therapy time and resources to craft cards and letters for family and friends outside of prison.

Hinson explained that these patients are their own harshest

critics. While the focus may be to color on the inside of a circular mandala in order to reduce one's heart rate, they may be preoccupied with going outside the line and when this happens. "They think they have to tear it up, because they're very hard on themselves. These are people who have made lifetimes of mistakes, in their eyes. And they don't want to make any more" (Tackara, 2016).

At Rikers there are 11 therapists working under Achitoff, including Hinson, and they are teaching a variety of disciplines such as art, dance and movement, and eventually they hope to have therapists teaching music and drama. These are funded through the Department of Corrections, or the DOC, through the efforts of New York City's Health and Hospitals Corporation, which is classified as a public benefit corporation. These programs are offered to the men, women and adolescents of the Rikers inmate population. Most of the inmates at Rikers are awaiting sentencing or serving sentences of less than a year.

According to the two art therapists, a majority of the patients participating in art therapy suffer from some sort of PTSD, as well as anxiety or depression. Rikers Island has a bad rep for their lack of abolition of solitary confinement for inmates under 21 years of age, which led to the issue of the suicide of 22-year-old Kalief Browder. Kalief completed his three-year stay at Rikers, beginning when he was 16, and spent nearly two of those years in solitary confinement.

Renee Obstfeld, an instructor in the art therapy programs at NYU and SVA, says that the conditions of solitary confinement can often mirror the conditions that many inmates experienced during their childhoods. Most of the trauma experienced by these inmates is attachment-based, meaning that typically these inmates grew up in childhood homes with a lot of abuse and violence. Most of their relationships were based on dominance and submission, intimidation, and coercion and secrecy.

Not only is this type of abuse psychologically damaging, but it can also be physically traumatizing since it causes the fragmentation of certain neuro-sequences the brains develop over time. These help people to adapt to any series of social situations. In a normal situation where one has a heightened state of arousal and vigilance, the ability for someone who has experienced this type of abuse to be flexible and adapt to these scenarios can become neglected.

People who experience this abuse also tend to the self-preservation of their emotions and vulnerability. By participating in art therapy, the effects of this abuse can be mitigated to restore the neuro-structures, enabling patients to regulate their emotions. This regulation can also be obtained by the making of choices of what art supplies to use, to calm and stimulate them, including the choice of colors as well as other artistic options.

The author of this editorial was unable to speak to patients directly or able to quote them specifically due to HIPPA regulations. However, Hinson did share some of their testimonial handwritten letters she received from the patients she had worked with:

> "I love our Tuesday, Thursday, and Friday sessions. Sometimes I could be in a really pissed off mood then ill realize I have art therapy and my whole mood changes. When I do color, I put my all intro those paintings." – Patient 1

> "Art means a lot to me, it reminds me of my childhood and being with my son. We colored all the time I just want [you] to know that it is very relaxing, it puts me in a good mood and it brightens up my day when Hinson comes. The pictures the markers, everything." – Patient 2.

Art can often give rise to a lot of emotions and memories. Even through this occurrence, the art therapists still attempt to reiterate the importance of not revisiting one's past traumas. Because art therapy is typically conducted in a group setting, it's important to highlight that hashing out one's trauma is more typically suitable for one-on-one sessions rather than group sessions.

Revisiting and unleashing trauma in a group setting is not only counterproductive but can also cause a chain reaction in upbringing someone else's traumatic experiences. Another reason to steer away from visiting past traumas in a group setting is that there is a certain level of trust and vulnerability when a group of people are with one another 24 hours a day every day. The goal of art therapy isn't to achieve all that, but rather to build or reestablish trust and understanding with oneself and with one another.

Success in art therapy can look different for every inmate. Usually, according to Hinson, it's found in mini-victories and breakthroughs, be it sharing materials with one another during sessions to completing a work over the course of a few sessions. In one inmate's case, the inmate was reluctant to participate in art therapy, but eventually came around and then stepped up to lead and instruct other inmates about the rules for group sessions.

"A woman who, through unlocking her creativity, realizes she's not an inherently dark person is a woman better equipped to step back in society—so is a patient who learns the value of the group's primary rule: to respect one another," reported Hinson. Some crucial goals and rules for art therapy include the maintaining of respect as well as containment. Containment is an important aspect, especially in an environment as unsafe as prison. It is important to maintain mechanisms of control not only of oneself, but of one's surroundings as well.

Some patients may be so mentally ill that containment is their only goal, rather than completing projects. It's more about allowing space for peace for the inmate than the work produced. Arguably one of the most important examples of containment is the storage of each inmate's artwork in a manila folder. While they may desire to hang it in their cells with the use of a little toothpaste, art and décor can be considered contraband and thus be confiscated by guards during cell searches. With the containment of artwork in each inmate's folder, one can go back and grow it from session to session, rather than hiding it in a cell.

One of Hinson's patients perceived herself as a dark person. However, she found herself filling in black lines with swirling patterns, encircling a woman's seemingly joyful face with colors of all shades of purple, orange, yellow, and blue. The work was seen by the patient as a self-exploratory piece in which she was able to find emotions of joy in her past and present self.

Another patient of Hinson's was incarcerated at the age of 17. She used collage work in order to work through her gender and sexual identity. In her work, there was a magazine image of an androgynous man wearing glitter makeup on their face with handwritten questions along the border asking "Beautiful?" "Hideous?" "What Are You?" "Who Are You?" (Tackara, 2016).

The therapists at Rikers Island are trained to navigate through sensitive dynamics and emotional responses. This can include avoiding conversations like, "What would you be doing if you were outside these walls?" because even a sense of almost-freedom, such as time in the rec yard, can be overwhelming to the inmates. It is important to recognize that these inmates are often not just to be seen as criminals, but also as human entities in which society has failed in one way or another.

Inmates who are patients in these art therapy programs find some form of humanization in the contact and relationships they not only form with themselves, but with one another—as well as their therapists. Hinson avoids researching her patient's cases in depth in order not to succumb to seeing them strictly as inmates, while also avoiding judgment and trepidation. One of the main pillars of psychotherapy is that the relationships formed between patient and therapist provide a model for how relationships should work in the real world, and this is most certainly achieved in art therapy.

One important factor about the relationship between the therapists at Rikers Island and the inmate patients is the placement of strict boundaries. For starters, this means that there needs to be a healthy means of ending the relationship once the inmate leaves the facility. The termination of these relationships can be proven difficult with an inmate's potential history of negatively ended relationships in the past.

However, with healthy boundaries and the knowledge that therapists will not remain friends with inmates after their sentence, negativity is alleviated some that can stem from terminating the relationship. By keeping these boundaries in place during the entire duration of the relationship, sudden changes in coming to and leaving the island can be more easily validated when they happen without warning. The expectation of the outcome is stated from the very beginning.

Some of the inmates in Rikers Island go on to pursue their art therapy at organizations such as Artistic Noise in Harlem "which helps released young prisoners transition back into society through art therapy" (Tackara, 2016). The importance of these programs both in and out of prison are high in not only the reintegration of inmates to society, but also the decreased mental illness and stigmas that are associated with mental illness in the prison system. Often when states go looking for budget cuts, the benefits of these programs can go unseen or unnoticed. The results that Achitoff, Hinson, and the other therapists see make it clear that more programming would not only be beneficial but is needed in state prisons. According to the Prison Policy Initiative there are over 2.3 million incarcerated men, women and adolescents in our country today, many of which are serving a sentence that is not their first.

EDMOND, OK COUNTY JAIL

Art therapy is not only found in educational programs but also in the desire to create by inmates during their free time, often within their cells. Throughout the history of jails and prisons, as long as there have been inmates, there has been an expression of creativity through "the endless production of wall murals, graffiti, effigies, adornments, decorative envelopes, and tattoos—to mention a few" (Hanes, 2005).

Many of the inmates have to rely on the resources around them that may not be considered traditional art supplies, as certain tools like pens and scissors may be security hazards. Instead, inmates may turn to using soap, toothpaste, toilet paper, magazines, and food pigment to entertain their creative ideas, for "where there is a creative passion, the resident will find a suitable material" (Hanes, 2005). Most of the time, the most readily available medium is a standard graphite pencil.

How is this not used as a potential weapon, you may ask? Pencils sold in commissary are kept to a length of two inches or less, so that in the event it was used as a harmful tool, it wouldn't do much damage. Throughout the course of this article's development and research, four common themes were discovered in the artwork of inmates which are time, escape, anger, and redemption. This particular jail only allowed observation of male inmates. Though the environment was poorly lit, photographs were taken of several anonymous art pieces.

Time is something that will always be of concern to inmates. Unlike a prison, jail staff often does have structured activities to help inmates pass what they call "dead time" (Hanes, 2005), and inmates, having no idea how long their time in jail will be, are fortunate to have even the shortest amount of time with access to a television or an outdoor basketball court. Inmates have nothing but time on their hands, as most of them can be in jail from days, weeks, or even years depending on the complexity of their cases and how backed up the court system. One of the drawings referring to this theme was a pencil sketch of a hot drink with the phrase, "#hots and a cot, that's all you got," referring to the notation that jails are only required to provide necessities such as a place to eat and sleep (Hanes, 2005).

Escape is not referring to the art of escaping the jail, but rather transporting one's mind to another world where the daily trials associated with incarceration are not present. The second figure in this article is a four inch by three-inch island scene that appears to be behind the torn away cinder blocks that make up the jail walls. Not only is the creator using this piece to represent his solitude, but also the escape the chaos of jail to the roaring seas where the viewer can find a peaceful escape filled with bliss and tranquility.

Anger and rage are not uncommon emotions when it comes to an inmate's newfound loss of freedom. It's no surprise that jails culture is often a hostile, vulgar, or harsh environment. The next figure discussed in the article is the words "Fuck you" etched in the plexiglass of a cell door. Not only does this image show aggression that inmates possess, but it also serves as a warning to "unwanted visitors" (Hanes, 2005). Why is this important to inmates? With an overwhelming amount of emotion and hostility, art provides inmates with a safe way of expressing their anger and aggression rather than taking it out on staff, other inmates, or even themselves.

One of the most frequently found images in this particular county jail was the Christian cross, not only being used to represent one's faith or repentance, but also a representation of suffering, humiliation, and atonement—as well as transformation. The cross "denotes the mercy of God giving redemption for the sins of man. It alludes to the crucifixion and the endurance of suffering. The cross may also represent the sign of victory over evil and life over death" (Hanes, 2005). The next figure was created by forcing toilet paper into a screen protecting a cell window, and portrays a steeple-like structure, where the three crosses of Calvary are found within.

SUMMARY

Overall, we know that the American prison system plays a large role in the culture of American society with a population of more than 2.3 million inmates, ranging in criminal activity from theft to murder to violent and nonviolent drug crimes. In addition to their preexisting mental health conditions, there's no wonder as to why there are so many different behavioral problems that inmates face. Art therapy is a program that can benefit inmates on a number of levels and has been a subject of research for nearly the past three decades.

Through qualitative as well as quantitative research, we have been able to see that prisoners who participate in this program see a wide range of benefits, including, but not limited to, improved attitudes and behavioral issues, greater willingness to participate in regular classroom educations, an increased feeling of self-worth and value, and better social relationships with other inmates as well as with prison staff and even members of an inmate's family and community. Overall, the main goal of art therapy is not just to improve these previous issues for inmates, but to prepare them for successful reintegration back into their communities after they are released from their imprisonment.

By allowing inmates to form these better connections to the communities where they will soon reside again, we give them hope and encouragement to want to better themselves, not only for personal reasons, but for their families as well. It gives them hope that a life of crime isn't the only thing they are capable of as individuals, and it gives the members of the community the opportunity and ability to see these men and women as more than a number and as a person outside of the crimes they have committed.

Research has shown us that there are not only sociological and physical benefits of art therapy, but that there are psychological benefits as well. With mental illnesses being a prominent factor in the lives of many incarcerated inmates, many of the prison's resources and a lot of money goes towards housing and providing care to these inmates. Not only do they need resources such as medication, but also, due to many behavioral issues they face, they require solitary housing. Art therapy is a practical resource for inmates suffering from mental illness since it gives an emotional outlet to a lot of different side effects of common illnesses such as depression, anxiety, and PTSD.

Recidivism is another issue for many inside the American prison system, and by teaching the inmates life skills not only to cope with their emotions, but also how to give them talents and capabilities outside of a life of crime is not only bettering the community as a whole but is also helping to keep men and women out from behind bars.

REFERENCES

Brewster, L. (2014). The Impact of Prison Arts Programs on Inmate Attitudes and Behavior: A Quantitative Evaluation. Justice Policy Journal, 11(2), 1-28.

Brinkman, Katelyn. "INCARCERATION AND IDENTITY: AN EXPLORATION OF ART THERAPY WITH INMATES." Concordia University, The Department of Creative Arts Therapies, 2017, pp. 1–78.

Carroll, H. (2016, September). Serious Mental Illness Prevalence in Jails and Prisons. Retrieved November 17, 2020, from https://www.treatmentadvocacycenter.org/evidence-and-research/learn-more-about/3695

Colorado College History Department. (2016, August 05). Art Therapy. Retrieved November 17, 2020, from https://sites.coloradocollege.edu/hip/art-therapy/

Gussak, D. (2007). The Effectiveness of Art Therapy in Reducing Depression in Prison Populations. International Journal of Offender Therapy and Comparative Criminology, 51(4), 444-460. doi:10.1177/0306624x06294137

Hanes, M. J. (2005). Behind Steel Doors: Images from the Walls of a County Jail. Art Therapy, 22(1), 44–48. https://doi.org/10.1080/07421656.2005.10129462

"John Wayne Gacy's Paintbox." Crime Museum, Natalee Holloway Resource Center, 2017, https://www.crimemuseum.org/crime-library/artifacts/john-wayne-gacys-paintbox/

Keller, B. (2016, March 10). Seven Things to Know About Repeat Offenders. Retrieved November 17, 2020, from https://www.themarshallproject.org/2016/03/09/seven-things-to-know-about-repeat-offenders

Nemade, R., Ph. D. (1995). Biology of Depression - Neurotransmitters. Retrieved November 17, 2020, from https://www.gracepointwellness.org/5-depression-depression-related-conditions/article/12999-biology-of-depression-neurotransmitters

Thackara, T. (2016, July 27). For Rikers's Most Troubled Inmates, Art Offers Hope. Retrieved from https://www.artsy.net/article/artsy-editorial-for-rikers-s-most-troubled-inmates-art-offers-hope

Wagner, W. (2020, March 24). Mass Incarceration: The Whole Pie 2020. Retrieved January 21, 2021, from https://www.prisonpolicy.org/reports/pie2020.html

Worrall, J., & Koines, M. (1978). Arts in Corrections: A Summary of Project CULTURE and a Handbook for Program Implementation [Scholarly project]. In American Correctionsl Association. Retrieved 2020, from https://www.ncjrs.gov/pdffiles1/Digitization/58266NCJRS.pdf

Www.rtor.org, (2020, July 29). Creativity and Recovery: The Mental Health Benefitsof Art Therapy. Retrieved November 17, 2020, from https://www.rtor.org/2018/07/10/benefits-of-art-therapy/

Meghan Cubbison is from Ottawa, Kansas. She has been part of the Vox Fortis select ensemble, a member and vice president of Theta Phi Alpha Sorority, and a member of Chi Alpha. Meghan majored in applied psychology with a concentration in criminal psychology. She plans on returning to OU in the fall to complete her master's degree in forensic psychology before going on to work as a behavioral health specialist in a prison.

LUKE GRAHAM

PREFACE

One of the key realizations I've had in my time at Ottawa is how diverse other individuals points of view and beliefs are. Someone can be presented with all the evidence of the Earth being spherical, but nonetheless, they may still believe the Earth is flat. I could describe to you how Ottawa has prepared me for a life of significance, but nonetheless, your personal belief on what a life of significance is may actually differ. For example, a considerable number of Hollywood characters depict a significant life in a way that glorifies more their possessions than their character.

Typically, these characters have a good job that pays well and has some meaning to it and have encountered some kind of a struggle in the past that has gotten the individual to this point. It's all surface, however, and it is more about their possessions in life (i.e. house, car, job). Yet, some characters begin as cold-hearted and selfish but after some dramatic event they realize the mistakes in how they are living. These kinds of character arc usually end with a change of heart, propelling them into a life focused on maximizing the relationships around them.

Where this hypothetical character's arc ends is the place that aligns with how I view a significant life. To me, a life of significance is focused on creating meaningful relationships. The best way for me to explain how Ottawa has helped prepare me for a life that I see as significant is by telling you my story.

Entry on 12/04/2020

I first arrived in Ottawa in the fall of 2018. I had arrived about a week before classes were scheduled to start for a required orientation week, which was expected for all incoming freshmen. When we arrived at the first activity, all the students were separated into their orientation groups, which ranged from 15-25 complete strangers. I belonged to the orange group and once called, we were told to meet outside for some get-to-know-you games. There I was, in a big circle, being told by two older Ottawa students (our leaders) to talk about myself and meet the other orange group members. Grudgingly, everyone began to mingle; after all, all of us were going to be together for the next week.

The rest of the week was spent almost entirely with orange group, adhering to the schedule full of activities, such as magicians, improv groups, and those long and boring informational meetings. Orientation week concluded with a day trip to Worlds of Fun, an amusement park in Kansas City. All the students were allowed to venture out on their own or in groups and encouraged to let loose. I broke away with a few people from the orange group and proceeded to have one of the best days of my life. However, that was the last time the orange group ever gathered as a whole, because once classes started and everyone's schedules changed, I was unable to see everyone very often.

This was the first time Ottawa had prepared me for a life of significance. I was able to meet and become emotionally connected with a handful of people who, without Ottawa's assistance, I would never have known. Orientation introduced me to some of my forever friends and gave me some of my most pleasant memories.

Entry on 08/20/2018

I was placed in Martin Hall with three golfers and two athletes who participated in track and field. When I arrived, my roommate Trey was already unpacking his things. Trey was a tall kid, naturally skinny but also toned, so I could tell he was still working out. He was wearing a pair of rectangular glasses that fit his face, and had a Napoleon Dynamite style haircut, which Trey was rocking. He was quiet at first, but if you started a conversation with him, he had no trouble speaking. We talked for a little bit, getting to know each other, before orientation activities began.

My nights during orientation were spent getting to know Trey and this progressed into daily interaction, which turned into going to dinner together, which blossomed into a strong friendship. We bonded over video games, movies, fusbol, music, TV shows (*Sherlock* was our favorite), and our common goals were aligned. Trey was that ideal freshman roommate who no one ever seems to receive. It was a friendship that was basically handed to Trey and me on a platter.

Out of all the people Ottawa could have roomed me with, I was assigned with one my future best friends. Trey helped me mend a broken heart, made me laugh when I was down, and helped me greet every new day with a smile. Our relationship seemed like fate, even if Ottawa randomly assigned us that room. I owe Ottawa for Trey as an addition to my life.

Entry on 05/30/2019

Shortly after school began, we both decided to join DECA, which was a club on campus focused on preparing students for interviews and solving business problems and how to present those solutions.

This is where I met Max. Max was the one who recruited Trey and me, and then he gradually became one of our closest friends. Trey and I had gotten so close to Max that we both attended his wedding this last fall.

One of the main reasons Trey and I joined DECA was for the competition side of things. Every year DECA has state and national competitions, and that year's national competition was being held in Orlando. The national competition was set for the middle of April. Trey and I decided to compete together, obviously, and we ended up winning at state. At nationals, Trey and I, the dynamic duo, did not make it past the first round. To be frank, we did horrendously.

Yet, that trip brought me closer with Trey, Max, and the rest of my classmates. The trip also provided an incredible amount of networking opportunities and skills. This was another convenience provided by Ottawa to where I was able to grow deeper in the relationships around me and seek new ventures that introduced me to new meaningful relationships.

Entry on 04/21/2019

Before I finished my freshman year, my economics advisor, Russ McCullough, invited me to an all-expenses-paid trip to FEEcon, a conference in Atlanta. This conference focused on economics, the environment, and growing into one's shoes. Once again, this trip provided me with an absurd amount of networking and close connections with other students my age.

Entry on 06/17/2019

My sophomore year started in similar fashion to the first one. I was once again in Ottawa a week before classes for orientation, except this time I was an orientation leader. I wanted to give my group the same experience I had, one full of new friendships and growth. This is where I met Collin, who quickly became one of my favorite kids and close friends—but more on that later.

This year I was living in Bennett Hall because that is where I was assigned for my new resident assistant job. Bennett was similar to Martin Hall with the suite-style living, but the main difference is there are only two bedrooms and one bathroom. Trey ended up having to leave the school for financial reasons and I was expecting to have a new roommate, but that person never showed up. After about two weeks of living on my own (and loving it I might add), one of my teammates named Luke moved in with me.

Luke and I bonded early over our common sport, namely tennis, and our name of course. Our room consisted of all players from the tennis team. Luke squared in one room and Erik and Isaac in the other. The four of us played ping pong together, video games, spikeball, basketball, and lived life together. The four of us slowly started to become better friends with a group of women—Alexis (who goes by Lex), Alicia, and Carmen. The group began by playing Wii games such as Just Dance or Mario Kart, then it turned into hanging out on weekdays, then weekends, and then major holidays.

This group grew even more when Collin (you remember Collin, right) and his roommate, Lawson, joined in on our shenanigans. We all started to consider each other as family, at least according to our Snapchat group chat entitled "Family + Distant Cousin." Collin was the distant cousin. Around this time, Lex and I started to become extremely close friends, and the irony of the situation is that she was in my orientation group. Our relationship has been something unique.

She was originally telling people on campus we were siblings, which of course everyone believed at first. There are definitely times where she tries to act like an older sister to me, even though I am older, but sometimes that tough love is needed. This "family" has been one of my biggest blessings, from helping each other with homework to encouraging someone who is down in the dumps, or even when someone has passed out on the bathroom floor (inside joke). This is a group of people I immensely cherish. Thank you, Ottawa, for somehow bringing all of us together.

Entry on 05/15/2019

Quickly into second semester, Jay persuaded me to join the fraternity on campus, Phi Delta Theta. This fraternity is not the typical fraternity seen on the news—not at all. First, they lacked official recognition of being a fraternity, for the sake of a small campus not providing a lot of numbers.

Second, there was no house for students to live in, another aspect that did not jive with the stereotypical fraternity. Third, it was a dry fraternity, meaning no alcohol, which corresponds directly with school policies (so you know we are not making the news). Jay encouraged me to invest my time in the fraternity because he thought I could really do something positive for us and the community.

Shortly after pledging, I was elected president, which led to delivering a speech at our installment as an official chapter of Phi Delta Theta. What an accomplishment for Jay and the rest of my brothers that was! Jay did all the hard work, and I got to enjoy the payoff, but I was determined to not let it go in vain.

My greatest accomplishment as president was organizing our annual Phi Delt 5K. This was a charity run through which students and the public could donate money to receive gifts. Our charity was Live Like Lou which is a nonprofit organization that raises money for research and support for ALS, amyotrophic lateral sclerosis. The gifts were blue and white rocket stickers for a $5 donation; a sticker and t-shirt with a unique design of a sticker design on the front pocket and moons on the back side with sponsors logos for $20; or $50 could get someone the sticker, t-shirt, and a two-feet-long challenge coin thanking them for their donation to Live Like Lou. We ended up raising over $3,000 from that event.

During that time while I was working on the 5K, I was networking in the community and creating relations with businesses, getting Phi Delta Theta's name into the City of Ottawa. Yet more importantly, I was creating stronger bonds with my brothers. For example, I became extremely close with one of my brothers, Brady. He was our treasurer at the time so he really helped me on the financial side of things during the 5K.

This led to us helping each other with homework since a lot of our classes overlapped, which eventually led to him throwing me a party for my twenty-first birthday this past week. In short, it all comes back to Ottawa's decision to allow Phi Delta Theta to come on campus, which led to me having a family of brothers and memories I can never share, and friendships I will honor forever.

Entry on 01/31/2021

Sophomore year ended early. Thanks, COVID.

Entry on 03/18/2020

My junior/senior year began amidst a global pandemic. I was an orientation leader once again but most of it was virtual, and the events we did have in person were short and socially distanced. Due to this, orientation made less of an impact on me, which in turn most likely meant less impactful for the incoming freshman. I retained my resident assistant job and my coworkers were the bomb.

Every semester RAs are required to arrive a little early to school for training. This training includes school policies, mental health awareness talks, and how to deal with almost every other situation. Let me tell you, most of these training seminars were boring, but the other RAs really made the time enjoyable. Also, one of the benefits of being an RA is that I always have someone who can relate to the stress and busyness the position creates.

Entry on 08/06/2020

Sadly, Luke had to transfer schools as well for financial reasons (hint, hint Ottawa). Despite going zero for two on maintaining a roommate, I was determined to make the most of the situation. That summer, I recruited one of my hometown buddies to come to Ottawa with me to play tennis and be my roommate. His name was Blake who I have known since we were both ten or eleven so that made it an easy transition becoming roommates. At this time I was no longer living with Erik or Isaac, but two freshmen named Jonathan and Logan. Blake, Jonathan, and Logan were adopted into "the family" and Logan became Lex and my little brother.

Everyday had potential chaos in that first semester of my last year. Quarantines were being handed out left and right and it became difficult to meet new people. Thankfully, I was able to have a group of friends that cared about me and helped me maintain my sanity.

Entry on 11/24/2020

My first semester ended and Logan had to leave (yes, financial reasons). Blake ended up moving out because he was twenty-one and could live off campus. That does not make me oh for three because he still attends here, right? Blake moving out meant that I *had* to convince the resident director to let me live by myself (no way I could lose another roommate). My begging and pleading resulted in me in getting a mega-bed, which is just two beds pushed together. It's much cooler this way.

The group remains intact, but it has grown. At this point, the group is as follows; Luke squared, Erik, Isaac, Lex, Alicia, Carmen, Trey, Collin, Lawson, Kayla (who Trey and I hung out with freshman year), Abi (Kayla's roommate), Logan, Jonathan, and Blake. There is a potential new family member, my new suitemate, Austen, who has been putting forth great effort to get to know Lex and me. Now you are caught up with where I'm at.

The final chapter of my time here at Ottawa is yet to be written with a few months remaining and I know when I leave that my time will have been significant, not because of any momentous action, but because of the lives I've touched and the people I've grown to know. Ottawa has prepared me for a life of significance by giving me people I call family, and by giving me opportunities to meet, grow, and love people.

Paused on 01/31/2021

Luke Graham is the son of Anthony Graham and Brenda Walker. He was born and raised in the country and suburbs of Tulsa, Oklahoma. He is a third-year senior participating in DECA and the new PPE-League here on campus. Luke is a resident assistant and also a member of the Ottawa tennis team. He was a double major in accounting and economics and is preparing to intern this summer while applying for graduation schools. Luke graduated in May of 2021.

ABIGAIL MEYER

NOTE FROM THE AUTHOR

A central theme to a liberal arts education is learning to examine a subject from multiple sides, evaluating different arguments and forming one's own opinions from that research. Religion can be a difficult concept to grasp, and the Bible is sometimes difficult to understand and then formulate your own beliefs. This is the final paper I wrote for an LAS course, called "Issues in Science and Religion." During this class, we looked at key arguments that divide science and religion and discussed how those differences could be reconciled—if possible. This course required me to expand my thinking in ways that were uncomfortable at times, though rewarding in the end.

For the final paper, we were asked to choose a topic relating to science and religion that we found interesting. My topic for this paper was "Biblical Hermeneutics," which is the science of biblical interpretation. I am proud of this paper and believe it represents my status as a Top Scholar because I was able to explain a complicated process in a way that is accessible to an average person, utilizing examples from the Bible to support my point. What's more, it helped me learn some applicable skills whilst reading the Bible, helping me in my own faith journey. I hope you enjoy it!

BIBLICAL INTERPRETATION: THE COMPONENTS AND PRINCIPLES OF BIBLICAL HERMENEUTICS

I would like to preface this paper by saying that biblical interpretation is a complicated concept. There are many different possibilities for interpretation and differing opinions regarding how it should be done. Interpreting the Bible is something I have personally struggled with, knowing what is true and should be taken literally as opposed to something that is meant to be figurative. I decided to take an objective approach while researching this subject, and the most helpful thing I came across was the study of biblical interpretation or hermeneutics.

My research outlined different opinions related to biblical interpretation, as well as provided a guideline for how interpretation should be approached. Throughout this paper, I will thoroughly discuss the four categories of biblical interpretation—literal, moral, allegoric, and anagogical interpretation—along with the implications of each. I hope to shed light on why biblical interpretation is important and help refine my beliefs and interpretation in the process.

Biblical hermeneutics is, as stated before, the science of biblical interpretation (*Encyclopædia Britannica*, 2020). The intent of hermeneutics is to discover the author's original goal in writing the Scriptures. Throughout history, there have been many debates concerning the best or most accurate way to interpret Scripture, and one of the main factors that played into that is scientific discovery.

Each of the authors we read throughout the semester showed how science and religion differed and offered suggestions as to how they can be reconciled. Some of the main arguments the authors put forward were heliocentrism and the beginning of the universe. Heliocentrism was a major debate in the era when Galileo lived, around the time of the Protestant Reformation. Galileo and other scientists before him were beginning to discover key evidence about a sun-centered world that contradicted what the Bible said—or how it had been interpreted.

This caused the Catholic Church to issue a decree stating that nobody could interpret the Scriptures in a way that contradicted the Church's interpretation (Blackwell, 1998, p. 27). This became a problem for the scientists who were discovering new things about the world and, although the decree was at some point lifted, the struggles between science and religion have lasted on through the years.

Another clear example of how some theories disagree with science comes from the creation story and how it conflicts with the scientific evidence that evolution and theories of the Big Bang have provided. If God created the world in seven days roughly 10,000 years ago, how can we account for the fossils we have found dating back billions of years ago? This leads to theories such as one called BioLogos presented by Francis Collins, which essentially suggests that evidence pointing to the existence of evolution and the Big Bang are valid, yet God could be the instigator of it all (Collins, 2007). This would suggest that, while the Bible is true and is God's inspired word, a passage that many read with a literal interpretation would now have to be read and thought of figuratively. This is where the problem of interpretation comes, in my opinion, because how does one decide what passages of the Bible to take figuratively and which to take literally? The process presented by hermeneutics may be helpful in helping the average believer navigate the process of interpretation.

Before we talk about the principles established by hermeneutics, let's discuss the categories of hermeneutics that have been proposed and utilized throughout history along with their implications. There are two general interpretations of Scripture: literal and spiritual, and the spiritual can be further broken up to include moral, allegorical, and anagogical (*Encyclopædia Britannica*, 2020). These interpretations do not have to be independent or exclusive of each other and can apply to different parts of the Bible.

First, let's look at literal interpretation, which is the approach that the Bible should be interpreted according to the "plain meaning" intended by the authors. It looks at the historical context of the text and the grammatical construction of the words in order to obtain the meaning of the Scripture (*Encyclopædia Britannica*, 2020). Literal interpretation accepts and understands the obvious use of figurative language that is used throughout the Bible, such as in Jesus' parables (Ice, 2009).

Most people who choose a literal approach to biblical translation believe that all historical events recorded in the Old Testament were factual, including all the lineages and miracles. The same can be said for the New Testament, including the Gospels (Matthew, Mark, Luke, and John) and the letters that Paul and other apostles wrote to the people in different locations. When parts of the Bible are meant to be taken figuratively and are clearly stated that way, such as the Psalms or Proverbs, then the figurative language is considered. The same applies to Jesus' parables ("What is Biblical Literalism?", n.d.).

There are some advantages and disadvantages of using this approach exclusively. One advantage is that provides the reader the ability to remain objective throughout the reading of Scripture. Reading it the way the authors intended it or wrote it to mean can provide the reader some security in the belief that they are not interpreting it incorrectly. Literal interpretation is the interpretation practiced by most evangelical denominations, and it is good because it considers historical context and authorial intent (Christian Publishing House, 2017).

There are some drawbacks to this approach, however. Depending on the person reading the Bible, it may or may not be clear what passages are intended to be taken as figurative language. The Psalms and Proverbs can clearly be seen as poems and other literary forms; however, it is unclear which other ones should be read figuratively. If passages, such as the creation story found in Genesis, are taken literally by the reader, there are some clear contradictions with scientific findings. The creation story does not speak of or mention evolution or the Big Bang, so readers are likely not to trust those scientific findings or may be confused about which to believe.

The next category of biblical hermeneutics is the spiritual, and one of the subsections is moral interpretation. Individuals who apply a moral interpretation of the Bible often read it and interpret ethical lessons from passages of the Bible that do not have those lessons explicitly stated (*Encyclopædia Britannica*, 2020). Often it involves reading "between the lines" in order to find application of the Scripture to daily life (Bible Society, 2016). There is an example of this in the Bible where it states,

> "For it is written in the Law of Moses: 'Do not muzzle an ox while it is treading out the grain.' Is this about oxen that God is concerned? Surely he says this for us, doesn't he? Yes, this was written for us, because whoever plows and threshes should be able to do so in the hope of sharing in the harvest" (1 Corinthians 9:9-10, NIV).

In these verses, Paul interprets a verse that was written in the Old Testament and finds an application of the Scripture to life in the New Testament (Bible Society, 2016). Moral teachings can also clearly be seen throughout Jesus' parables in the New Testament, where he would often take everyday situations that his followers are familiar with and intertwine a lesson.

The next subsection of the spiritual interpretation is allegorical. Allegorical interpretation of Scripture involves a deeper level of meaning that is not immediately seen or explicitly stated. Often, it comes in the sense of foreshadowing in the Old Testament to the New Testament (*Encyclopædia Britannica*, 2020). For example, in Genesis chapter 22, God told Abraham to take his son Isaac and use him as a sacrifice. Abraham almost did this, but God stopped him and commended him for listening to God without question (Genesis 22:1-19 NLT).

This image of a father sacrificing his son may be seen as foreshadowing Jesus being sacrificed for all in the New Testament. It is not explicitly stated, but after reading about Jesus' sacrifice, this symbolism and many others can be seen in the Old Testament pointing to Jesus and events to come. People who use an allegorical mindset are able to see various meanings in passages of Scripture that are not immediately seen without further reflection.

Finally, the third component to spiritual interpretation is anagogical. Anagogical interpretation reads Scripture in terms of eschatology, which is the study of the end times (Oxford Reference, n.d.). Anagogical interpretation allows the reader to see examples within the Bible that point to eternity in Heaven. Some of these examples come from Jesus' parables.

An example of this can be found in Mathew 25:31-46 when Jesus was talking about separating sheep from goats. Jesus said that the sheep, who he herded to the right, will enter the Kingdom of God because they obeyed his commands and loved others the way Jesus told them to. The goats, on his left who did not obey these commands, were sent to eternal punishment (see Matthew 25:31-46, NLT). This is a clear example of Jesus referring to the day of judgement during the end times ("Four Senses of Scripture," n.d.). Other examples are not as clear, such as the parting of the Red Sea being symbolic of believers on the path to heaven through baptism (Catechism of the Catholic Church, 1997).

These three subunits—moral, allegorical, and anagogical—make up the spiritual categories of hermeneutics. Like the literal interpretation, there are advantages and disadvantages to using this method exclusively. Some advantages are that it allows the reader to be able to find and understand all possible meanings behind a passage of Scripture, allowing it to better relate to them in their daily life ("Rise of Allegorical Interpretation", n.d.).

Another advantage is that it allows some reconciliation of scientific discovery with Scripture. Rather than reading the creation story in Genesis as Adam and Eve being the literal first humans ever created, it may be that Adam and Eve are embodiments and representatives of humanity, and God used the story to make it easier to understand and more accessible for the average person (Walton, 2015).

If God were to tell the writers all about hydrogen and nitrogen and the exact mechanism God used to create humanity, many would be confused and not as likely to believe the Scripture. By simplifying it into the story of Adam and Eve and the six days of creation, God enabled His followers to accept that God is the creator of all and to learn a moral lesson about the fall of humanity.

There are disadvantages to solely following Scripture in a spiritual sense, however. By creating one's own interpretation of the Scripture and discovering a meaning behind it, there is a chance that the method could be abused. The individual may adapt the meaning of Scripture in a way that was not originally intended in order to suit their own personal beliefs or agenda (GotQuestions.org, n.d.). There would need to be scriptural basis for each interpretation in order to justify the allegorical meaning. Otherwise, anybody could interpret and preach about something that was not in the Bible or had little scriptural foundation.

As you can see, there are both benefits and downfalls to both the literal and the spiritual interpretation when they are both used exclusively. How then can a reader make sure they are interpreting Scripture in the way it was intended? The response is quite simple, actually. By reading the Bible in both spiritual and literal ways, the reader can get the most out of the reading while ensuring they are not interpreting it falsely. A method for doing so is proposed within the science of hermeneutics.

While reading Scripture, there are different principles that can be applied to each passage in order to get the correct historical context. There are many different sources and different guidelines for hermeneutics, but they all attempt to accomplish the same thing—interpreting the Bible in the way it was originally intended. This set of guidelines is presented by James Davis who is a project manager for Bible.org, but there are others that may suit a reader's preference. These principles can be facilitated by a study Bible or other credible sources.

The first principle is that interpretation of a passage must be looked at through the eyes of the author, not the eyes of the reader. The reader must look at who the author was and their context, as well as the historical and cultural context of the time (Davis, 2013). The Bible shouldn't be read through the lens of the 21st century, because that is not when it was originally written. The knowledge of the culture and that of the world should be considered.

The second principle is that the interpretation must be looked at in context of the passage. The context of the Scripture will determine its meaning, so individual verses should not be interpreted on their own without looking at the entire passage (Davis, 2013). The third principle is to take the Scripture literally, but still allow for the use of figurative language. Verses that use "like" or "as," or have hyperboles are figures of speech.

For example, Matthew 17:20 says, "Truly I tell you, if you have faith as small as a mustard seed, you can say to this mountain 'Move from here to there,' and it will move. Nothing will be impossible for you" (Matthew 17:20, NLT). It does not mean that faith is measurable in the sense of the millimeters that a mustard seed is, or that one can tell a mountain to move and it literally will. Rather, this is a verse talking about how faith in God can help the reader get through difficult times in their life (Plumptree, 1907).

The fourth principle is to use the Bible to interpret itself. There are many different passages that speak about the same concept, so if one is difficult to understand, the reader can look at simpler ones in order to gain a better understanding. Also, if an Old Testament passage is being interpreted, context from the New Testament can help the individual understand the reasoning and the overall purpose of the Old Testament passage (Davis, 2013).

The fifth principle is to distinguish interpretation from

application. As stated earlier, biblical passages should be read in context of the historical times. However, application can be used in order to relate the interpretation to the modern world. For example, the concept of loving your enemies from Matthew 17 can be applied to a co-worker or a friend who upset you (Davis, 2013).

The next and sixth principle is to distinguish between Old Covenant and New Covenant passages. Certain rules and laws that were established in the Old Testament under the Old Covenant that were not repeated in the New Testament do not still apply. For example, the passage about not being able to wear clothes of two different fabrics from Leviticus is not applicable under the New Covenant created through Jesus (Davis, 2013). If it was stated in both the Old Testament and New Testament, then it still applies to everyday life.

Finally, the seventh principle is to be aware of the type of literature the passage is in. There are a lot of different types of literature in the Bible ranging from narratives, poetry, and parables to gospel and apocalyptic (Davis, 2013). Poetic passages use a lot more figurative language, and parables teach a lesson to the readers. Gospel passages relate to the story of Jesus, and each author had a specific audience they are writing to. This can help explain subtle differences between each author's narrative of Jesus. Revelation is an apocalyptic message, and it is often difficult to understand and interpret because it talks about the end times in a type of literature not common today (Davis, 2013). It may be helpful to read it with the use of a commentary or study Bible, and to seek to understand the overall message of the book or passage rather than look for meaning in individual verses.

Overall, the principles discussed within hermeneutics in general are not an exact science, but can be used and are beneficial when interpreting Scripture. The goal is to help readers be able to interpret Scripture in a way that is accurate so they can better understand what God is revealing to them. I believe that while this does not solve everything in terms of possible confusion around interpretation, it can provide a method that leads to a deeper understanding of God's Word and will.

Interpretation of the Bible is something that is extremely important for believers, because it is often a main foundation for their faith. Applying all seven principles to each passage in Scripture will not be easy. By practicing hermeneutics and taking it slowly, interpretation may turn into an easier process that will enhance the reader's faith, and hopefully bring them closer to God.

WORKS CITED

1 Corinthians 9:9-10. (n.d.). Retrieved from https://www.biblegateway.com/

Anagogical. (n.d.). Oxford Reference. Retrieved from https://www.oxfordreference.com/view/10.1093/oi/authority.20110803095410406

Blackwell, Richard J. *Science, Religion and Authority: Lessons from the Galileo Affair*. Marquette Univ. Press, 1999.

Catechism of the Catholic Church. (2020). Retrieved from https://www.catholicculture.org/culture/library/catechism/index.cfm?recnum=467

Christian Publishing House. (2020, January 10). BIBLICAL INTERPRETATION– A Literal-Historical-Grammatical Approach. Retrieved from https://christianpublishinghouse.co/2017/08/19/biblical-interpretation-a-literal-historical-grammatical-approach/

Collins, F. S. (2007). *The language of God: a scientist presents evidence for belief*. New York: Free Press.

Four Senses of Scripture. (n.d.). Retrieved from http://www.catholiccrossreference.com/biblestudy/four-senses-of-scripture/

GotQuestions.org. (2016, October 19). Allegorical Interpretation. Retrieved from https://www.gotquestions.org/allegorical-interpretation.html

How can the Bible be interpreted? (n.d.). The Bible Society. Retrieved from https://www.biblesociety.org.uk/explore-the-bible/bible-articles/how-can-the-bible-be-interpreted/

Ice, Thomas D., "Literal vs. Allegorical Interpretation" (2009). *Article Archives*. 62. https://digitalcommons.liberty.edu/pretrib_arch/62

Plumptree, E. H. (1905). Matthew 17. In C. J. Ellicot (Ed.), *Ellicott's Commentary for English Readers*. Retrieved from https://biblehub.com/commentaries/ellicott/matthew/17.htm

The Editors of Encyclopaedia Britannica. (2020, March 10). Hermeneutics. Retrieved from https://www.britannica.com/topic/hermeneutics-principles-of-biblical-interpretation

The Rise of Allegorical Interpretation Commentary - A Testimony of Jesus Christ. (n.d.). Retrieved from https://www.biblestudytools.com/commentaries/revelation/introduction/the-rise-of-allegorical-interpretation.html

Tyndale House Publishers. (2012). Genesis. *Teen life application study Bible: New Living Translation. Teen life application study Bible: New Living Translation*. Carol Stream, IL.

Tyndale House Publishers. (2012). Matthew. *Teen life application study Bible: New Living Translation. Teen life application study Bible: New Living Translation*. Carol Stream, IL.

Walton, J. H. (2015). *The lost world of Adam and Eve: Genesis 2-3 and the human origins debate*. Downers Grove, IL: IVP Academic, an imprint of InterVarsity Press.

What is biblical literalism? (n.d.). Retrieved from https://www.compellingtruth.org/biblical-literalism.html

Abigail Meyer is a senior from Princeton, Kansas. She was a member of FCA, the Whole Earth Club, and Residence Life. Abigail majored in biology and graduated in May of 2021. Following graduation, Abigail plans to pursue graduate school to become a speech-language pathologist.

ALLISON RIVERS

As a requirement for the biology degree, I was given the privilege of designing and performing a senior research project during the fall semester of my senior year. My project consisted of collecting microorganisms, growing them in a laboratory setting, and identifying which microorganisms are present in bowling balls. This project has important value because it gave me the chance to find a career that would be enjoyable and gave me the motivation to change my decision and pursue a master's degree program in medical laboratory science. I am providing a modified presentation that explains my senior research project.

ABSTRACT:

The objective of this project is to be able to accurately collect, grow, and identify a mixed culture of bacteria found in a personalized bowling ball. This project is also idealized to be able to effectively identify the difference between bacterial cultures and contaminants. Based on the performance of multiple tests performed on the bacteria grown, there can be an accurate identification found in the finger hole drillings of a personalized bowling ball.

Bacteria is found in any public spacing available to human contact and is easily transmitted through airborne activity and touch. Once biochemical testing was completed throughout a total of five trials, the identities of the unknown microorganisms were determined. *E. coli, C. fruendii, S. flexneri, S. sonnei, S. sonnei, P. aeruginosa* were all identified throughout the trials during the experimental periods.

INTRODUCTION:

Bowling is a sport growing in popularity that has multiple physical and mental aspects, such as a stress relief and increasing social abilities (The Bowling Universe, 2017). Although there have been studies performed on the effects of the human aspect, the studies on the spread of bacteria through a bowling alley is limited. Common bacteria found throughout the public settings are *Bacillus spp., S. aureus,* and *E. coli* (Tekerekoğlu, Yakupogullari, Otlu, Duman & Gucluer, 2012).

Since this project is based on a popular attraction that includes an exercise activity and concession found in Ottawa, the spread of bacteria can be found from multiple ways such as the contamination from either food, urine, or wounds (Kleyn, John, Bicknell, and Oller, 2012). With the means of different contaminations, it is likely to see other bacteria such as *S. epidermis, P. Vulgaris, Pseudomonas, Klebsiella, Salmonella,* and *Shigella* along with multiple other possibilities (Kleyn, John, Bicknell, and Oller, 2012). The purpose of this project is to be able to accurately and successfully identify the bacteria found in the mixed cultures collected in the finger drillings of a bowling ball.

MATERIALS AND METHODOLOGY:

This experimentation will begin with the preparation of Brian Heart Infusion (BHI) slants to grow the collection of mixed cultures on day one (Center for Food Safety and Applied Nutrition, n.d.). The ideal process of a slant is to add about six mL to each tube and lay on a slant to harden for future testing. Two sterile swabs are dipped in distilled water and both the inside of the grips and around the edge of the grips are swabbed for the collection of microorganisms.

This process will be completed for both the left and right finger grips. Swab the plates in one direction and invert for incubation (Balootaki, Amin, Haghparasti, & Rokhbakhsh-Zamin, 2017). Based on the process presented in the reading, the swabs were swiped across the BHI slant in a zig-zag motion. BHI slants that were inoculated are incubated at 37° for twenty-four hours.

Once the incubation of bacteria was completed, a Gram Stain was performed to identify the size and shape of the colonies. Gram Staining is a key technique to establish microorganism's ultrastructure. If there is a cell wall present, the organism will appear purple because of the retainment of the crystal violet, while gram-negative organisms will appear pink (O'Toole, 2016). The Gram Staining process is important to identify and distinguish the difference between organisms based on the possible presence of a cell wall.

The process was to examine the streak plates and identify the colonies formed on each plate and record observations. For the organisms that grew and isolate a significant amount, I performed another Gram Stain for confirmation of the cultures grown. he colonies selected by isolation will continue with the tests that were earlier prepared to perform on the different types of fermentations. I incubated the test tubes for 24-48 hours (checking at the 5-hour mark for H2S production) at 37°. After incubation, Bergey's Manual of Determinative Bacteriology was used to accurately determine the identity of the microorganism by the completed tests.

BIOCHEMICAL TESTS

Eosin Methylene Blue (EMB) is a differential and selective medium to gram-negative organisms. This test is used to isolate and differentiate coliforms and fecal coliforms (Tankeshwar, 2013). If the test is positive, the organisms will appear metallic-green. This is a confirmation that the organism ferments lactose.

Hektoen Enteric agar is a differential and selective medium to gram-negative bacteria, and the bile salt concentration is high enough to inhibit intestinal bacteria, such as *shigella* and *salmonella*. A positive test will appear in one of two ways: if the organisms' ferments lactose and/or sucrose, the colony will appear orange, and non-fermenting colonies will appear blue green. Hydrogen sulfate production will form a black precipitate in the middle of the colony (Kleyn, Bicknell, & Oller, 2012). With having an unknown related to food poisoning, this test is important in identification.

Triple Sugar Iron (TSI) slant is a differential medium that shows sugar fermentation. This test involves the fermentation of glucose, sucrose, and lactose. Glucose is in the bottom of the tube, while sucrose and lactose are located throughout the slant. Phenol red indicator is used and appears red throughout the tube. If there is fermentation present, then the tube will turn yellow with the possibility of bubbles if there is a gas produced. Along with a change in color, if hydrogen sulfate is produced, there will be black coloring throughout the tube (Tankeshwar, 2013). Red coloring is labeled as "K" and yellow is "A" to designate positive and negative results.

Simmon's Citrate Utilization is a test used to distinguish the members of the Enterobacteriaceae family based on by-products. Citrate utilization is used to distinguish between coliforms that naturally occur in soils and fecal coliforms that indicate fecal contamination (Tankeshwar, 2013). The agar contains pH indicator bromthymol blue and has an initial pH of 6.9. If the pH increases, the indicator will turn from green to a deep blue.

Sulfur Indole Motility (SIM) agar deeps are used where the organism is stabbed into the agar and growth will appear cloudy in the tube. Kovacs reagent is added to the agar and a red ring will identify indole positivity; yellow is negative, and formation of hydrogen sulfide will create a black precipitate (Kleyn, Bicknell, & Oller, 2012).

Phenylalanine Deaminase Test (PAD) is a differential medium that determines if the organism can produce phenyl pyruvic acid from phenylalanine deaminase. If this test is positive, the medium will turn dark green in coloring (Kleyn, Bicknell, & Oller, 2012). This is a useful test to distinguish the members of the Enterobacteriaceae family, specifically differentiating *Proteus* and *Providencia*.

Xylose Lysine Deoxycholate (XLD) is a selective medium for the isolation of *Salmonella* and *Shigella* species commonly found in clinical specimens and food samples. These pathogens are differentiated by non-pathogenic lactose fermenters and non-pathogens that do not ferment lactose or sucrose. Degradation of xylose, lactose, and sucrose will generate acid products, causing the medium to change colors

GRAM STAINING OF A CULTURE

Once the incubation of bacteria was completed, a Gram Stain was performed to identify the size and shape of the colonies. Gram Staining is a key technique to establish microorganism's ultrastructure. If there is a cell wall present, the organism will appear purple because of the retainment of the crystal violet, while gram-negative organisms will appear pink (O'Toole, 2016). The Gram Staining process is important to identify and distinguish the difference of organisms based on the possible presence of a cell wall.

Examine the streak plates and identify the colonies formed on each plate and record observations. For the organisms that grew and isolate a significant amount, perform another gram stain for confirmation of the cultures grown. The colonies that were selected by isolation will continue with the tests that were earlier prepared to perform a test on the different types of fermGram Staining of a Culture

Once the incubation of bacteria was completed, a Gram Stain was performed to identify the size and shape of the colonies. Gram staining is a key technique to establish microorganism's ultrastructure. If there is a cell wall present, the organism will appear purple because of the retainment of the crystal violet, while gram-negative organisms will appear pink (O'Toole, 2016). The Gram Staining process is important to identify and distinguish the difference of organisms based on the possible presence of a cell wall.

Examine the streak plates and identify the colonies formed on each plate and record observations. For the organisms that grew and isolate a significant amount, perform another gram stain for confirmation of the cultures grown. The colonies that were selected by isolation will continue with the tests that were earlier prepared to perform a test on the different types of fermentations. Incubate the test tubes for 24-48 hours (check at the 5-hour mark for H2S production) at $37°$. After incubation, Bergey's Manual of Determinative Bacteriology is used to accurately determine the identity of the microorganism by the completed tests.

RESULTS:

Trial 1:

Trial 1 began with a successful growth of bacteria on a BHI slant for both the left and right finger grips. Once the gram stain was completed, observations under the microscope included both gram-positive and gram-negative bacilli shown in the left finger grip. In the right finger grip, gram-negative bacilli were observed.

Trial 2:

During Trial 2, there was no bacterial growth present on the BHI slant to perform biochemical tests. One possibility conclusion for the lack of growth of microorganisms is the lack of use of the bowling ball preventing the ability of transfer of microorganisms from the operator to inside of the finger grips.

Trial 3:

Trial 3 had a successful growth of bacteria on a BHI slant for both the left and right finger grips. Once the Gram Stain was completed, observations under the microscope included gram-positive cocci. In the right finger grip, gram-negative bacilli were observed.

Trial 4:

Trial 4 had a successful growth rate of microorganisms on the BHI slants. The Gram Stain on the left finger concluded the presence of Gram-negative cocci. The Gram Stain for the right finger was also conclusive to Gram-negative cocci.

Trial 5:

During Trial 5, there was no microorganism growth present on the BHI slant to perform the selected biochemical tests. The limit of growth could have been caused by the lack of use of the bowling ball preventing the ability of transfer of microorganisms from the operator to inside of the finger grips.

DISCUSSION:

For the identification of the left finger grip in Trial 1, the Gram-negative bacilli gave the first indication to the microorganism being identified as *E. Coli*. The EMB test was the next indication of *E. coli* due to the green color production in the slant that is personalized to this microorganism. The XLD slant, Mannitol Salt, and the TSI have gas produced in the butt of the tube were all further indications the microorganism in the left finger grip could be identified as *E. coli*. *E. coli* is commonly transferred through fecal contaminants and can be easily transferred throughout public areas.

For the right finger grip in trial 1, the important identification factors included the ability to produce sulfide during the TSI test. The Simmon's Citrate, Mannitol Salt, and Hektoen Enteric tests were all positive tests that led the identity to *C. fruendii*. This microorganism is also lactose fermenting, which concluded the results from the EMB testing. The conclusions of the tests determined the identity to be *C. fruendii*. This bacteria can also be transferred through fecal contaminants along with contaminated and recreational water sources.

Trial 3 began with the left finger grip with the main factor including Simmon's Citrate concluding in a negative result. This led the identification to be *S. flexneri*. Mannitol Salt concluding in a positive test also led to the identification of this microorganism along with the organism being non-fermenting.

The right finger of trial 3 is concluded as *P. vulgaris* due to the Gram Stain appearing negative and the TSI test appearing acidic throughout the butt and tube along with other tests concluding negative such as the Simmon's Citrate. This microorganism is commonly found in soil, recreational water sources, and fecal matter, and is commonly known to cause UTI's.

The identification of the left finger of Trial 4 was concluded as *S. sonnei*, which is a Gram-negative bacillus that is non-motile along with being Simmon's Citrate negative and production of Lactose. *S. sonnei* is found to be ingested through the use of contaminated or recreational water sources. It is commonly found in industrial areas with a higher chance during pandemics.

The right finger of Trial 4 was concluded as *P. aeruginosa* due to the TSI slant depicting mostly the same color, but the butt appearing a slightly more orange coloring than the rest of the slant. Mannitol Salt, Simmon's Citrate, and Hektoen Enteric were also positive tests that concluded the identity of the microorganism as *P. aeruginosa*. This microorganism thrives in moist environments and can be commonly found on the skin. It can be easily transferred through human contact, found in many water sources, and is found on many fresh fruits and vegetables.

Allison Rivers is a senior from Gulfport, Mississippi. She is a member of the bowling team, Biology Club, student government, and is a member of the Campus Activities Board and a resident assistant. Allison majored in biology and graduated in May of 2021. Allison plans to continue her education by applying to attend a master's program in biomedical sciences.

HANNAH O. SAUCEDA

SPORT SKILL ANALYSIS: POLE VAULT PLANT, JUMP, AND TURN

INTRODUCTION

In pole vaulting, one of the most important factors in your jump revolves around how you plant your pole, jump off the ground, and twist your body off of the ground. These contributing factors are often unnoticed by beginners. In fact, most beginners believe that when you are jumping off the ground, you are simply trying to propel yourself over the bar by sheer force. The reality of the skill is that it is a combination of the planting of the pole into the box, how you jump from the runway, and finally, twisting your body over the bar. The main objective of this skill is to ensure that you get your body high enough over the bar in order to clear it.

There are a few different phases/key points that make up the entirety of this skill:

- **Phase 1: Planting of the pole**
    1. Rotating the pole from below to above the athlete's shoulder
    2. Firmly pushing end of the pole into the box
    3. Absorbing the shock of the force by bending the elbows
- **Phase 2: Jumping from the runway**
    1. Pushing off on foot from the runway
    2. Swinging the legs up to propel them above the shoulders
    3. Pulling up on the bar while the athlete is in the motion of swinging their legs
- **Phase 3: Twisting body over the bar**
    1. Rotating the body 180 degrees
    2. Pushing back on the bar once the descent onto the mat begins.

Phase one begins once the athlete rotates the pole from the

lower half of the transversal plane to the top half and ends as soon as the tip of the pole hits the stop board. When approaching the box, the athlete will begin the transition of moving the pole from below the waist to above their head. Ideally, the athlete should have their arms extended out in front of their body, locked out, and ready for the tip of the pole to enter the box.

The takeoff foot should be directly under the top hand at takeoff. This maximizes the distance between the top hand, the ground, and the pole angle at takeoff. This position puts the athlete in preparation for the next phase. If you were to take a freeze frame of an elite vaulter as soon as the tip of their pole reaches the edge of the box, the angle from athlete to box would be around 18 to 21 degrees.

Phase two begins once the pole starts to bend as a result of the force acted upon it from the weight of the runner and the speed of the approach. This phase ends once the athlete is in the motion of pulling themselves up on the pole, while simultaneously swinging their legs to begin the rotation of the hips for the final phase. The vaulter should attempt to remain right side up immediately after takeoff by keeping the body in an extended position. This will keep the mass of the vaulter closer to the pole's axis of location.

When the athlete feels the pole start to bend, their elbows should be bending with it. This will help reduce the stress and the impact of the blow put on their arms. The athlete should also be bringing the pole to the non-dominant side of their body, while pulling up to assist in the swing.

The swinging of the legs is the most important step because it aids in the momentum of the athlete. The quality of the swing is determined by the degree of the horizontal displacement of the athlete's shoulders and hips. All these steps should be done in one continuous motion to aid in the fluidity of the jump.

Phase three begins mid-swing as the athlete starts the hip rotation to bend their body and push their center of gravity over the bar. The phase ends when the athlete has released the pole and begins their descent to the mat. As the "swinging phase" ends, the athlete's hips should be in full extension to stay in line with the pole. When the torque (or hip rotation) is beginning, the athlete would ideally position their pole diagonally against their body and as a result, have momentum and resistance to turn their stomach towards the bar. During the final stages of clearance, after the athlete has released the pole, the vaulter should make sure to lift and rotate their elbows outward to avoid contact with the bar.

There are a variety of muscles from different groups that help assist when performing the vault. These muscles are used to either accelerate or decelerate the skill, stabilize, and/or neutralize the body during the skill.

Upper Body Muscles

Muscle Name	Used For
Pectoralis Major/Minor	Stabilizes body upon planting in the box
Deltoid	Used to plant the pole into the box/pull body up on pole and over the clearance bar
Trapezius	Used to plant the pole into the box/pull body up on pole and over the clearance bar
Rhomboid Major and Minor	Assists in stabilizing the plant into the box
Teres Major and Minor	Assists in stabilizing the plant into the box
Subscapularis	Assist in stabilizing while pulling body up on the pole/over the bar
Supraspinatus	Assist in stabilizing while pulling body up on the pole/over the bar
Biceps/Triceps	Used to plant the pole into the box/pull body up on pole and over the clearance bar/stabilizes and helps absorbs shock of impact into the box/pushing pole away when over the bar
Extensor Carpi Radialis Longus	Providing hand and wrist strength to help grip the pole

All of the muscles listed in the tables are what assist a vaulter throughout their jumps. These muscles work simultaneously to change the horizontal position and speed to vertical.

MECHANICAL ANALYSIS

The pole vault in track and field is an event that combines both power and speed. When competing at an elite level in this event, athletes must have a heavy focus and awareness on their equilibrium since these different factors are what contribute to a successful jump. As the athlete begins to sprint down the runway, they build up kinetic

Abdominal/Hip/Butt Muscles

Muscle Name	Used For
Gluteus Maximus/Minimus/Medius	Helps maintain upside down body position
Piriformis	Helps maintain upside down body position
External Oblique	Used to swing legs upward, hold body position, and turning body over the clearance bar
Internal Oblique	Used to swing legs upward, hold body position, and turning body over the clearance bar
Transverse Abdominis	Used to swing legs upward, hold body position, and turning body over the clearance bar
Rectus Abdominis	Used to swing legs upward, hold body position, and turning body over the clearance bar
Iliopsoas	Used to help swing the legs upwards when jumping from runway to the air
Sartorius	Used to help swing the legs upwards when jumping from runway to the air

energy. This energy dissipates once the athlete begins the takeoff phase (the very first jump from the runway into the air). At the point of maximum height, the kinetic energy that has been built up is at zero.

In order to maximize the vault height, the athlete bends their body over and around the bar. Doing this keeps their center of gravity underneath the bar. In turn, this means that the bar can actually be placed above the maximum height reached by the center of mass.

Another factor in the athlete's equilibrium is stability. In order to perform a strong and stable jump, the athlete must have adequate core strength. This factor gives the athlete the ability to manipulate their center of mass, thus allowing them to maximize their potential jump height.

An additional advantage of having a strong core is how it is related to hip flexion and hip rotation, both of which are necessary attributes for the athlete to turn from a vertical standpoint back to a horizontal one. Focusing on the little details of the equilibrium is what distinguishes elite athletes from the amateurs.

CONCLUSION
COACHING/TEACHING TIPS

Whether or not an athlete is a beginner or experienced, a coach should teach with some of the following guidelines:

1. The vaulter should always understand that sufficient pole speed will not only aid in the success of the jump but will also help ensure the safety of the jumper.
2. During the early stages of teaching, coaches should emphasize the importance of horizontal movements.
3. Coaches should always push vaulters to focus on vault efficiency rather than excessively high hand grips. A vaulter should be able to jump at least 15 inches above the hand grip. If this can't be done, technical problems exist.

POLE SELECTION:

When selecting a pole, an athlete should keep some of the following things in mind:

1. The vaulter should not be using a pole that has a body weight standard less than their actual body weight.
2. The only way you can accurately gauge a pole is when the vaulter is using correct technique.
3. An athlete should choose a pole that can be gripped anywhere from 6 to 18 inches from the top.
4. Lastly, the vaulter should understand the flexion characteristics of the pole. The stiffer the pole is, the higher the potential of the vault is. However, a stiffer pole can lead to technical efficiency harder to achieve.

COMMON ERRORS:

When learning to vault, there are a few common mistakes that most athletes make:

1. **Incorrect step.** Whenever the athlete's last left foot lands, it should be directly beneath their top hand.
2. **Late plant.** The pole plant should be occurring in the last 2 to 3 steps of the approach. The pole must be all the way above the athlete's head, in full extension, before the pole hits the back of the box.

3. **Locking out the plant too long.** The left arm must be brought in eventually to achieve proper rock-back. The arms can stay locked out throughout the row until the left arm becomes parallel with the body, then the left arm travels up the body (bending at the elbow) and stays very close to the body in order to get vertical.

REFERENCES

Edouard, P., Sanchez, H., Bourrilhon, C., Homo, S., Frère, J., & Cassirame, J. (2019, August 21). *Biomechanical Pole Vault Patterns Were Associated With a Higher Proportion of Injuries*. Frontiers. https://www.frontiersin.org/articles/10.3389/fspor.2019.00020/full

Nice, K. (2000, September 22). *How Pole Vaulting Works*. HowStuffWorks. https://entertainment.howstuffworks.com/pole-vault3.htm

Physics Of Pole Vaulting. (n.d.). Retrieved November 25, 2020, from https://www.real-world-physics-problems.com/physics-of-pole-vaulting.html

Tian Yang, W., & Bo, W. *New Core Stability Strength Concept for Training Pole Vaulter*. Journal of Health Science. http://article.sapub.org/10.5923.j.health.20190901.01.html.

Hannah O. Sauceda is a graduating senior from Terrell, Texas and was a member of the Braves cross country and track and field team. Hannah majored in exercise science with a concentration in pre-allied health and graduated in May of 2021. Upon graduation, Hannah's plan is to attend graduate and medical school and then work as the head team physician in the NFL.

WILLIAM WALLACE

PREPARE FOR A LIFE OF SIGNIFICANCE

Significance is a tricky word that has a concrete meaning but is as unique to every individual as a snowflake is to a tree branch, and for a University to claim it prepares graduates for a life of significance, it must be careful to provide a significant, unique college experience for each student who attends. For this essay, I was tasked with describing how Ottawa University has prepared me for a life of significance post-graduation.

As a reference point as to the importance of this question to the Ottawa Scholar, the mission statement of the University is as follows:

> "Building on its foundation as a Christ-inspired community of grace and open inquiry. Ottawa University prepares professionals and liberal arts graduates for lifetimes of personal significance, vocational fulfillment and service to God and humanity."

From this mission statement, it would seem to the outsider looking in that the goal inherent in this statement is creating individuals inspired solely by Christ and his teachings. But to the student living the life, this statement takes on other meanings, meanings of challenging discussion, intensive introspection, and maintaining an open mind and an open heart for thought and growth. Significance lies in the eyes of the individual and the responsibility to create it lies on their shoulders, while the University is responsible to provide opportunity for experiential learning. Let's discuss this by highlighting examples and key words from the mission statement and examining them closely.

First, let's look at Ottawa's claim of being a body of "grace and open inquiry." When we think about the word *grace*, a few synonyms come to mind such as patience, understanding, and tolerance. Being a community dedicated to grace would mean that tolerance is at our core in every sense of the word—tolerant of other individuals, tolerant of other beliefs, and tolerant of other ideas. A tolerant individual does not look to the world through shaded lenses but allows for their lenses to be altered and adjusted after careful deliberation and open inquiry.

The reality of human experience in education is to ask questions about the nature of life and the physical world. These two terms, grace and open inquiry, are presented in this order not to create an alphabetical list of values that the University upholds, but to demonstrate the importance of these concepts working in tandem to create growth in the life of an individual. Without grace, exposure to new ideas will only lead to being closeminded and fearful, and without the ability to freely and confidently ask questions, an individual will not be able to relate these new ideas to themselves. When that occurs, growth towards significance will not take place. The emphasis of these two terms within the mission statement helps transition know-it-all high schoolers into lifelong learners. From my experience at Ottawa University, allowing yourself to ask questions is the best way to understand and find creative solutions to life's problems.

Another key phrase found in the University's mission statement is the bit about a lifetime of personal significance and vocational fulfilment. It is an obvious fact of life that people are unique, and not just unique in the notion of personality and preference, but also in what it is that makes them tick. While the technical definition of significance is "the quality of being worthy of attention; importance" (dictionary.com), the actual application of finding significance in life is a little more complex.

It requires an individual to sit down and decide for themselves where is it that they are, and where is it that they plan on going. Significance cannot be ordered or created, but instead must be discovered. Significance can be found in the fulfilment of the self, in the aiding in the suffering of others around you, in the advancement of human knowledge or experience, or in creating something that will supersede your physical existence.

While there are many other ways to achieve some sort of personal significance, finding fulfilment in vocation is the most impactful on the individual. Without a passion for the work one is doing, there seems to be no feasible way to do meaningful work. Ottawa University lives up to this expectation by not attempting to portray the world in a manner that may or may not be compatible with reality and hope the two line up. Instead, it propels its undergraduates into the process of exploring life and identifying places in which their efforts are both needed and impactful.

How this has materialized in my own experiences throughout my four years at this institution is the support I have garnered from my professors, mentors, and football coaches to step outside my comfort zone until I could find something meaningful with which I am comfortable. What that has looked like for me is the mentoring I have received from my professors to examine all aspects of engineering and technical work until I can find something that excites my passions and drives me to make an impact in that particular field of study. My professors have been looking beyond the classroom since I have arrived and have done nothing but spur me towards finding my passions and work towards something that has significance to me personally and to the people around me.

The concluding words of the mission statement of Ottawa University, "service to God and humanity" has a varying degree of importance to people but the general idea rings through. One of the easiest ways to find significance in a life is to make an impact on and through an organization or idea much bigger than an individual could ever be. Whether that's though charitable acts, generous donations, or the pursuit of relationship with a higher power, it is a nearly universal desire to work for something bigger than the self. While this is not the truth in every case, a good majority of the population does strive to find this form of fulfillment in life.

A side benefit to this way of seeking significance is surrounding yourself with individuals who share a common belief and or goal and then encouraging another human being to become the best version of themselves, which can be quite fulfilling. For Ottawa University this means pursuing meaning in some form of Christ-inspired service and teaching. Ottawa fulfills this promise made to the students by providing many opportunities every year for students to give back to the community through service and leadership and by also challenging students to reflect on what it means to be serving others and serving Christ through mandated Gospels classes and weekly spiritual development talks.

Another way in which this gets fulfilled has less to do with the actions of the University and administration but more with the people you meet. On this campus, I have personally been encouraged by many individuals to live a meaningful and conscious life though service to others and service to Christ. My best friends spend a staggering amount of time encouraging me to do my best in everything I do, as if I were working for someone greater than man, and something greater than myself, be that a deity or a cause. I cannot thank them enough for these reminders to live an intentional life. In some regards, these personal relationships I have developed with my peers have done more to help me strive towards a life of significance than anything else. My experiences have succeeded in nurturing this lifestyle going forward.

Finally, the declaration that Ottawa University encourages both 'professionals and liberal arts' students carries a certain amount of weight regarding the way in which Ottawa prepares students for a life of significance. Universities across the country are more than capable of churning out graduates who hold the technical skills and ability to perform tasks of unheard-of complexity. However, what sets Ottawa apart as a school that produces capable graduates is the emphasis that the courses place on all aspects of life.

As an engineering student, this has taken on the practice of developing my ability to problem solve. This does not mean my ability to sit down and work problems in the back half of a chapter in a textbook, but to investigate an open-ended need or problem and come up with an innovative and effective solution.

And to step back even more from the world of engineering and into my personal life, Ottawa University encourages its students to analyze all situations, problems, and vocations with the idea that what they are doing matters not only to them and the people around them, but also to future generations and culture as a whole. The University challenges us to think about the cultural, environmental, financial, and intellectual impact of our actions. While it seems unproductive and counterintuitive to require technical students like myself to take courses in philosophy and ethics, the correlations between and applications of these methods of thought are deeper than one would imagine and aid graduates in creating an impact in their chosen field of study.

This essay could not be complete without one minor suggestion from the author about the nature of the mission of Ottawa University. The first words of the second line of the mission statement is "Ottawa University prepares…" While most would agree that the mission statement previously mentioned has the best intentions for the development of an undergraduate student into a life of significance the responsibility for, this transformation falls on the student more than the University.

I have seen individuals come to this university without a solid understanding of their own goals and intentions and then fail to find some form of significance in becoming who they were meant to be. While I am no linguist, and the ways of the written word come better to me in the form of rants and hardly comprehensible sentences, the mission should read, to the effect, that Ottawa University provides students with the *opportunity* to create a life of significance.

The beautiful thing of attending a university is hardly found in the classroom where you are required to sit for six hours a day, but rather in the meaning you discover though relationship and personal effort. As I mentioned in my opening example about grace and open inquiry, significance cannot be ordered or handed down, but rather inspired. A student who attends Ottawa University will be given every opportunity in the world to discover a life of significance, but the responsibility lies on their shoulders to make it a reality.

Ottawa University has served me well in helping me find meaning in a life that could be defined as significant. I have learned that learning to approach the world with grace and open inquiry will allow me to become a lifelong learner outside of the classroom for the eventual betterment of humanity. Discovering passion will enable a student to pursue a study and vocation with the confidence that what they choose to do will be of significance to others. The best way to do that is to identify what it is that is important to you and how you can get there.

Ottawa has taught me that Christ-inspired service is a way in which an individual can find meaning and purpose in life, but that an ideology that goes unchallenged will grow stagnant and die. Challenging yourself to remember why it is that you believe and act the way you do is related to significance. Another encouragement from Ottawa has been to examine challenges and tasks from multiple perspectives to find solutions that have bigger and more significant implications.

While the University embarks on their mission to create graduates who live a life of significance, the responsibility ultimately falls on the student to prepare themselves during their time here for their future. While I have worked hard to allow my time at Ottawa to transform me into an individual with a life of significance, it has not always been easy. This process has come with its ups and downs but ultimately, I am encouraged with my path of life and thankful to the people I have met and the experiences I have had and shared with some amazing comrades, professors, and friends.

William Wallace is a senior from Strasburg, Colorado. He was a member of the Braves football team, Ottawa University Theater Club, and Ottawa University Campus Ministries. Will majored in engineering and graduated in May of 2021. Following graduation, he is planning on either pursuing graduate studies in mechanical engineering or beginning a career as a mechanical engineer.

CONCLUSION

As we close, I'd like to thank our Scholars and their families. Editing this book has been a pleasure and a blessing. With each volume, I find myself getting to know my students better, including scholars who I haven't had the pleasure of directly instructing for the first time. These young adults are impressive, their ambition is humbling, and their optimism is inspiring. They are a credit to this institution, their parents, and themselves. I am thankful and excited to spend more time with our returning scholars in the next year, and I wish the graduating scholars the best of luck. – Justin

www.ingramcontent.com/pod-product-compliance
Lightning Source LLC
LaVergne TN
LVHW051459070426
835507LV00022B/2848